BUMPEI BISCUIT

COMPILED BY
WENDY SILVER

VLAEBERG PUBLISHERS

CONTENTS

Foreword 3
Introduction 4
Biscuit barrel 6
No-bake 16
Jam biscuits 19
Dried fruit biscuits 23
Piped and pressed 27
Ginger and spice 32
Kiddies' treats 39
Citrus biscuits 44
Nutty biscuits 50
Chocolate and coffee biscuits 56
Savoury biscuits 63
Mixed bag 65
Cereal 69
Slices 72
Special occasions 75
Alphabetical recipe index 87

© Copyright Wendy Silver

All rights reserved

Published by Vlaeberg Publishers
P.O. Box 15051, Vlaeberg 8018, South Africa

ISBN 0-947461-13-2
First edition, first impression 1992

Cover design by Abdul Amien
Production and design by Wim Reinders & Associates cc
Setting and reproduction by Hirt and Carter (Pty) Ltd

FOREWORD

From the YF Kitchen-tested recipes in this book, you can prepare an endless variety of tantalising, easy home-made biscuits for family and friends. It takes only an hour, or less, to transform the most common kitchen ingredients into fragrant, spicy Oatmeal drops; fruit-flecked Florentines; or cheesy Juggler's sticks. We've also included a section of No-bake delights for the quick-mix set, who want a sweet treat without the heat.

So, beat up a batch without delay – sweet or savoury – few things bring on a smile as fast as a plate of home-baked biscuits or cookies: the smiles will linger, the biscuits won't!

Wendy Silver

WENDY SILVER
SENIOR COOKERY EDITOR, YOUR FAMILY

INTRODUCTION

Originally a simple substitute for bread, biscuits were made of flour and water and baked twice, hence the French name *Bis cuit*. This made them really dry and long-lasting, ideal in situations where regular baking was not possible, such as on board ship. The nearest modern equivalent is the water biscuit, neither sweet nor savoury, but usually served with cheese.

To vary the original recipe, other ingredients such as butter, sugar, eggs and flavourings were added and richer, sweeter biscuits were developed. Even so, true biscuits are still thin and crisp, and keep well if correctly stored.

Cookies should have a softer, more cake-like texture, but with American usage of the term "cookie", referring in fact to biscuits, the two names have become virtually interchangeable.

Most biscuits and cookies are easy to make but, as with all baking, they require accurate measuring of ingredients and minimum of handling to be successful. For each basic recipe, there are several others one can invent by varying the flavouring, shape or decoration.

PREPARATION
Roll out dough to an even thickness so that biscuits brown evenly, and try to keep shapes more or less the same size, so they all cook through. Place biscuits on a flat baking tray or sheet, preferably without sides, or with very low ones – high sides prevent proper browning. Use upside-down roasting-pans if you need extra trays. Most recipes will stipulate a lightly greased tray, but don't grease if the recipe doesn't ask for it. Similarly, you must line the tray with greaseproof or non-stick paper if called for in the recipe, otherwise the dough may stick to the tray. Lightly grease the tray with oil or non-stick spray, line with a sheet of paper, then grease again lightly.

BAKING
Preheat the oven before you start, to ensure the correct temperature is reached by the time you want to bake the biscuits. Bake biscuits on the centre shelf of the oven, and never overcook. They should not be too brown, rather just a pale golden colour.

COOLING
Normally biscuits should be transferred to a wire cooling rack as soon as they come out of the oven, but there are some, especially those sweetened with syrup or honey, which need to cool and harden on the tray for a minute or two before being moved. Always lay biscuits flat without overlapping or they will bend and become misshapen.

STORING AND FREEZING
Most biscuits and cookies keep well for up to two weeks if stored in an airtight tin. Layer with wax-paper and secure lid firmly. Store biscuits undecorated and always store soft and crisp ones separately. If any lose their crispness, pop them into a 180°C oven for five minutes and allow to cool on wire cooling racks before serving.

Biscuits and cookies keep well in the freezer for several months. They may be frozen in dough form, or baked and ready to eat.

Remember these points when freezing them:
☐ Remove all air from the container, seal, label and date.
☐ Baked biscuits may be frozen for up to four months, whereas the raw dough will keep for six months.
☐ Don't freeze iced biscuits.
☐ Pack baked biscuits carefully in boxes to avoid crushing.
☐ Thaw baked biscuits, still wrapped, at room temperature, one hour. Crisp up in warm oven for five minutes.
☐ Form biscuit dough into a 50 mm-diameter cylinder, wrap in clingwrap and foil before freezing, or pipe into shapes, open-freeze, then pack into rigid containers when firm and return to freezer.
☐ Allow frozen cylinder of dough to thaw for 45 minutes at room temperature before slicing and baking.
☐ Bake shaped biscuits straight from frozen, allowing seven to 10 minutes longer than time stated in recipe.

DECORATING
Biscuits and cookies can be topped with a soft butter icing, royal icing or glacé icing, or spread with melted chocolate. Use nuts, dried fruit, jam, vermicelli, *nonpareilles*, silver dragees, glacé cherries or angelica for additional decoration, or simply dredge with sifted icing sugar. Useful tools to make decorating easy are a small wooden board and sharp knife for chopping, a wire cooling rack for drying biscuits, a small palette knife for spreading icing or chocolate, and a pastry brush for dusting away crumbs or to brush a thin glacé icing over the biscuits. Piping bags with a variety of writing and decorative nozzles, and toothpicks or tweezers to pick up tiny decorations, are also necessary tools to give your biscuits a totally professional finish.

TYPES OF BISCUITS AND COOKIES
1 Bars and slices
They can be crisp, or soft and cake-like. They're easy to make: simply spoon or pour batter into a greased and lined, deep-sided baking tray and bake in one piece. Cut into fingers, bars or squares when baked.

2 Drop cookies
The dough is too soft and sticky to roll. It's placed by the spoonful on to a lightly

greased baking sheet. Some spread during baking to become thin, brittle biscuits, while others retain their shape and have a softer, cake-like texture when baked.

3 Shaped biscuits
The dough is soft, and is moulded by hand into sausage-shapes, pretzels, rings and so on. Handle quickly and keep hands floured to prevent sticking.

4 Piped and pressed biscuits

The mixture must be smooth, and soft enough to flow through a piping nozzle or biscuit-maker, but firm enough to hold its shape during baking. There is an endless variety of shapes one can make out of one basic dough just by varying the disc or nozzle.

5 Refrigerator cookies
These are crisp, thin biscuits made from a rich mixture which improves with keeping. An excellent stand-by for fresh biscuits in a hurry!

When required for baking, slice off thin biscuits from the roll of dough. If frozen, allow to thaw slightly before slicing and increase baking time.

6 Rolled biscuits
These biscuits are crisp. The dough is rolled out thinly on a floured surface and cut into shapes with a knife and template, or with a biscuit cutter. The dough must be firm and pliable – chill it well and then roll out between sheets of greaseproof or wax paper. Don't add

extra flour to stop it sticking – this will make the biscuits tough.

7 Unbaked biscuits
Breakfast cereal, biscuit crumbs, marshmallows or chocolate are usually the basis for these. The biscuits are either formed into shapes with the hands, or spread or poured into a greased and lined baking tray or lamington pan. They're cut into bars or squares when firm. Store unbaked biscuits in the refrigerator, but don't freeze.

BISCUIT BARREL

◀ Fruit-mince delight *(top)*; Crunchy chocolate bars *(bottom)*

CRUNCHY CHOCOLATE BARS

100 g butter *or* margarine, softened
150 g (300 ml) flour, sifted
100 g (150 ml) soft brown sugar

FILLING
25 g (50 ml) flour
3 ml baking-powder
15 g (37,5 ml) cocoa powder
50 g (62,5 ml) castor sugar
2 eggs, beaten
5 ml vanilla essence
100 g (312,5 ml) desiccated coconut

ICING
40 g (100 ml) drinking chocolate powder
50 ml hot water
25 g butter *or* margarine
200 g (385 ml) icing sugar, sifted
3 ml vanilla essence

Rub butter into flour, add brown sugar and work into a stiff dough. Press into greased 180 mm by 280 mm swiss roll pan. Bake at 180 °C, 10 minutes.

Filling
Sift together flour, baking-powder and cocoa, mix in castor sugar, eggs, vanilla essence and coconut. Spread carefully over base and bake 25 minutes. Cool in pan.

Icing
Mix chocolate powder with water. Beat in butter, icing sugar and vanilla essence until smooth. Spread icing over filling. When set, cut into bars.

Makes 32 bars.

FRUIT-MINCE DELIGHT

300 g (600 ml) flour, sifted
5 ml ground cinnamon
pinch of salt
180 g butter *or* margarine, softened
125 g (150 ml) castor sugar
1 large egg, lightly beaten
500 g jar fruit mincemeat
sifted icing sugar for dredging

Sift flour, cinnamon and salt into a bowl. Rub in butter until mixture resembles fine breadcrumbs. Stir in castor sugar and egg, form dough into a ball. Knead lightly until smooth, refrigerate one hour.

Cut dough in half. Grate half over base of 180 mm by 280 mm greased lamington pan. Press down lightly with the back of a spoon. Spread fruit mincemeat over base and grate remaining dough over top to cover completely.

Bake at 180 °C, 35 to 40 minutes or until golden brown. Dredge with icing sugar while still warm. Allow to cool on wire cooling rack, cut into squares.

Makes 12 to 16 squares.

BUTTER FINGER BISCUITS

300 g butter, softened
180 g (215 ml) castor sugar
400 g (800 ml) flour, sifted
pinch of salt
100 g (200 ml) cornflour, sifted
castor sugar for dredging

Cream together butter and castor sugar until pale and fluffy. Sift together flour, salt and cornflour, mix into creamed ingredients. Knead lightly.

Press into deep, greased 380 mm by 280 mm baking tray. Prick well with a fork and bake at 190°C, 25 to 30 minutes.

Remove from oven, dredge with castor sugar, and cut into fingers while still warm. Remove to wire cooling rack and allow to cool completely. Store in airtight container.

Makes 44 fingers.

▲ Kisses from Holland *(top)*; Scoop biscuits *(centre)*; Hawaiian biscuits *(bottom)*

KISSES FROM HOLLAND

250 g butter *or* **margarine, softened**
250 ml oil
210 g (250 ml) castor sugar
130 g (250 ml) icing sugar, sifted
2 eggs, lightly beaten
5 ml vanilla essence
600 g (1 200 ml) flour, sifted
5 ml bicarbonate of soda
5 ml cream of tartar
2 ml salt

TO DECORATE
desiccated coconut
chopped nuts

Beat butter and oil well, add sugars. Beat in eggs and vanilla essence. Sift together dry ingredients. Add to creamed mixture to form a wet dough.

Drop spoonfuls of dough into coconut or nuts, coating well. Shape into balls and place on lightly greased baking trays. Bake at 150 °C, about 15 minutes or until pale cream in colour. Remove to wire cooling racks to cool completely.

Makes 48.

SCOOP BISCUITS

225 g (280 ml) sugar
280 g butter *or* **margarine softened**
2 eggs, lightly beaten
170 g (280 ml) seedless raisins
55 g (140 ml) chopped nuts
360 g (720 ml) flour, sifted
15 ml baking-powder
2 ml salt

Cream together sugar and butter in a mixing bowl until light and fluffy. Add eggs, beat well. Stir in raisins and nuts. Sift together dry ingredients, add gradually to creamed mixture, beating well. Place walnut-sized spoonfuls on lightly greased baking trays.

Bake at 200 °C, about 10 minutes or until pale golden brown. Remove to wire cooling racks to cool completely.

Makes about 80.

HAWAIIAN BISCUITS

200 g (250 ml) sugar
125 g butter *or* **margarine softened**
1 egg, lightly beaten
190 g (375 ml) flour, sifted
5 ml bicarbonate of soda
5 ml baking-powder
2 ml salt
90 g (250 ml) rolled oats
80 g (250 ml) desiccated coconut
5 ml vanilla essence

Cream together sugar and butter until light and fluffy. Add egg, mix well. Sift together flour, bicarbonate of soda, baking-powder and salt. Beat into mixture together with remaining ingredients.

Roll dough into small balls and place on lightly greased baking trays. Press each ball down gently with a fork.

Bake at 180 °C, 10 to 15 minutes or until golden brown. Remove to wire cooling racks to cool.

Makes 36.

CARAMEL BISCUITS

500 g butter *or* margarine, softened
375 g (470 ml) sugar
397 g can full cream sweetened condensed milk
750 g (6 x 250 ml) flour, sifted
12,5 ml baking-powder
pinch of salt
10 ml caramel essence

Cream together butter and sugar until light and fluffy. Stir in condensed milk. Sift in dry ingredients, mix well. Lastly, add caramel essence, beat well.

Roll 5 ml amounts of mixture into balls, place on lightly greased baking trays. Press down with a fork (or spoon mixture into biscuit-maker and press out biscuits on to trays).

Bake at 180 °C, 12 to 15 minutes until golden brown. Transfer to wire cooling racks to cool. Store in airtight containers.

Makes about 240 biscuits (if using biscuit-maker).

STEP-BY-STEP BUTTER BISCUITS

BASIC DOUGH
120 g butter *or* **margarine, softened**
250 g (500 ml) flour, sifted
1 ml baking-powder
pinch of salt
180 g (215 ml) castor sugar
1 egg, lightly beaten
5 ml vanilla essence

Cherry buttons
one quantity basic dough
glacé cherries, quartered

Sugar pretzels
one quantity basic dough
20 g (12,5 ml) creamed honey
5 ml ground cinnamon
1 egg-white, lightly beaten

Jam daisies
one quantity basic dough
raspberry jam
sifted icing sugar

Chocolate and almond squares
one quantity basic dough
50 g (100 ml) ground almonds
melted chocolate

1 Cherry buttons
2 Sugar pretzels
3 Jam daisies
4 Chocolate and almond squares

1 **Basic dough** Rub butter into flour until mixture resembles fine breadcrumbs. Stir in baking-powder, salt and castor sugar. Make a well in centre of mixture, add egg and vanilla essence. Mix well to form a soft dough. Chill in refrigerator 30 minutes.

Makes 20 to 30 biscuits, depending on shape.

2 **Cherry buttons** Form basic dough into small balls, place on lightly greased baking trays. Flatten ball with a fork and top with a cherry.

3 **Sugar pretzels** Mix honey and ground cinnamon into basic dough. Shape mixture into thin, 180 mm-long sausage shapes. Form into pretzels. Place on baking trays. When almost cooked, remove from oven, brush with egg-white and sprinkle with sugar. Return to oven, bake a further five minutes.

4 **Jam daisies** Roll out basic dough to 5 mm thickness. Using a 50 mm fluted cutter, cut out bases. Then cut out an equal number of rounds using a smaller cutter. Using a very small cutter, cut out centres of second rounds. Place on baking tray. When cooked, dust rings with icing sugar and sandwich rings and bases together with jam.

5 **Chocolate almond squares** Mix ground almonds into basic dough. Roll out dough to 5 mm thickness. Using a sharp knife, cut out 50 mm squares. Place on baking trays. When cooked, dip diagonally in melted chocolate. Leave to set on wax-paper.

To bake
Place all biscuits on lightly greased baking trays. Bake at 200 °C, about 12 minutes or until pale brown. Place on wire cooling racks to cool. Store in airtight containers.

11

Clockwise from top: Chip biscuits; Custard kisses; Shrewsbury biscuits; Sour cream raisin biscuits

SOUR CREAM RAISIN BISCUITS

80 g butter *or* margarine, softened
10 ml finely grated lemon rind
210 g (250 ml) castor sugar
1 egg, beaten
300 g (600 ml) flour, sifted
3 ml bicarbonate of soda
pinch of salt
125 ml sour cream
100 g (170 ml) seedless raisins
80 g (250 ml) desiccated coconut

Beat butter and lemon rind in a mixing bowl, add castor sugar and egg, beat well until light and creamy. Sift in flour, bicarbonate of soda and salt alternately with sour cream. Mix in raisins. With floured hands, roll 5 ml amounts of mixture into balls, roll in coconut, place on lightly greased baking trays, leaving space between biscuits for spreading.

Bake at 180 °C, 10 to 15 minutes. Remove to wire cooling rack to cool.

Makes 32.

SHREWSBURY BISCUITS

250 g butter *or* margarine, softened
300 g (375 ml) sugar
2 eggs
600 g (1 200 ml) flour, sifted
10 ml baking-powder

Cream together butter, sugar and eggs until light and fluffy. Sift in dry ingredients, mix well to form a soft dough. Place in biscuit-maker, press out biscuits, or roll into small balls and flatten with a fork.

Bake at 180 °C, 15 to 20 minutes or until light brown. Cool on wire cooling racks.

Makes 60 to 70.

VARIATIONS
Almond, cherry and nut
Add 100 g (155 ml) chopped glacé cherries, 50 g (125 ml) slivered almonds and 5 ml almond essence to basic dough. This mixture, however, is not suitable for pressing through a biscuit-maker. Roll dough into 30 mm-diameter sausage shape, refrigerate 45 minutes or until firm. Cut into 5 mm slices, place on baking tray, bake as above.

Coffee nut
Add 10 ml instant coffee powder and 25 g (60 ml) chopped nuts to basic dough. Continue as above. This mixture is not suitable for the biscuit-maker.

Makes about 30.

CUSTARD KISSES

180 g butter *or* margarine, softened
65 g (125 ml) icing sugar, sifted
180 g (360 ml) flour, sifted
60 g (120 ml) custard powder

ICING
150 g (300 ml) icing sugar, sifted
warm water to mix

Cream together butter and icing sugar until light and fluffy. Sift in dry ingredients, mix well to form a dough. Fill biscuit-maker with mixture, press on to ungreased baking trays.

Bake at 200 °C, 12 to 15 minutes. Remove to wire cooling rack to cool completely.

Icing
Sift icing sugar into a bowl, add warm water to form a smooth, thick icing.

Sandwich biscuits together in pairs.

Makes 22 pairs.

CHIP BISCUITS

250 g butter *or* margarine, softened
400 g (500 ml) sugar
2 eggs
380 g (760 ml) flour, sifted
3 ml bicarbonate of soda
3 ml baking-powder
60 g (300 ml) crushed cornflakes
160 g (445 ml) rolled oats

Cream together butter and sugar until light and fluffy. Add eggs one at a time. Add remaining ingredients, mix to combine. Roll into walnut-sized balls, place on greased baking trays, press down with a fork.

Bake at 180 °C, 10 to 15 minutes or until golden brown. Remove to wire cooling rack to cool.

Makes 65.

CINNAMON SNAPS

250 ml oil
300 g (375 ml) sugar
2 eggs, beaten
330 g (660 ml) flour, sifted
pinch of salt
12,5 ml cream of tartar
5 ml bicarbonate of soda

COATING
80 g (100 ml) sugar
12,5 ml ground cinnamon

Mix oil, sugar and eggs in a large bowl, set aside. In another bowl, combine remaining ingredients, stir into oil mixture. Refrigerate 45 minutes.

Roll into walnut-sized balls. Combine sugar and cinnamon in a small bowl. Roll balls in cinnamon sugar.

Place about 50 mm apart on ungreased baking trays. Bake at 200 °C, 10 minutes or until lightly browned. Remove to wire cooling racks to cool.

Makes about 55.

Orange creams *(left)*; Cinnamon snaps *(right)*

ORANGE CREAMS

870 g (7 x 250 ml) flour, sifted
500 g (625 ml) sugar
2 ml salt
500 g butter *or* margarine, softened
4 eggs, beaten
10 ml cream of tartar
5 ml bicarbonate of soda
juice and rind of 2 oranges

ORANGE CREAM
260 g (500 ml) icing sugar, sifted
orange juice (from above)

Sift flour into a large mixing bowl. Add sugar and salt. Rub in butter. Add eggs, cream of tartar, bicarbonate of soda, orange rind and 100 ml of the orange juice. Mix to form a soft dough. Refrigerate one hour.

Place in biscuit-maker, press out shapes. Bake at 190 °C, 10 to 15 minutes or until lightly browned. Remove to wire cooling rack to cool completely.

Orange cream
Sift icing sugar into a bowl. Gradually add orange juice to form a smooth, creamy icing.

Sandwich cooled biscuits together with orange cream.

Makes 65 pairs.

QUICK-MIX BISCUITS

BASIC DOUGH
125 g butter *or* margarine, softened
150 g (180 ml) castor sugar
250 g (500 ml) flour, sifted
37,5 ml milk
20 g (12,5 ml) golden syrup

Place butter, castor sugar, flour, milk and syrup in a mixer bowl. Beat well until mixture forms a soft ball. Turn out on to a lightly floured surface, knead well.

Shape biscuits (see below), chill until firm. Place on ungreased baking trays and bake at 190 °C, 10 to 12 minutes. Leave to cool five minutes only, then remove to wire cooling racks to cool completely. Store in airtight containers.

Makes about 20 biscuits.

FLAVOURS
Orange or lemon Add finely grated rind of one orange or one lemon and replace milk with orange juice, or milk and 5 ml lemon essence.
Chocolate Replace 30 g (60 ml) flour with 30 g (75 ml) cocoa powder.

VARIATIONS
Spangles Divide dough into pieces, form into rolls about 100 mm long. Make 'S' shapes. Bake. When cold, drizzle a little glacé icing over biscuits and sprinkle with *nonpareilles* (100s and 1 000s).

Sunny circles Divide and shape dough into walnut-sized pieces. Flatten each slightly and make an indentation in the centre. Fill with 2 ml lemon curd or apricot jam. Bake.

Chocolate and orange marbles Knead together chocolate-flavoured and orange-flavoured doughs to give a marbled effect. Form into a 50 mm-diameter log. Wrap in clingwrap and chill. Cut into thin slices and bake.

Cherry garlands Roll dough into small rounds the size of marbles. Place five rounds together to form circles on baking trays. Cut glacé cherry in half. Place one half in centre of biscuit, slice remaining half into five thin slices. Place between each dough 'petal'. Bake. (125 g glacé cherries will decorate 20 biscuits.)

Sugared knots Divide chocolate-flavoured dough into small pieces, form into rolls about 150 mm long and carefully tie into knot shape. Bake. Sprinkle with castor sugar while hot.

Chocolate mint buttons Shape chocolate dough into 40 mm-diameter log. Wrap in clingwrap. Chill. Slice thinly. Bake. Decorate with green, peppermint-flavoured glacé icing when cold, and top each with a milk chocolate button (Smartie).

DATE-NUT RIBBONS

250 g (500 ml) flour
3 ml salt
1 ml bicarbonate of soda
180 g (250 ml) soft brown sugar
125 g butter *or* margarine
37,5 ml milk
1 egg, beaten

FILLING
150 g (250 ml) stoned dates, chopped
50 g (125 ml) walnuts, chopped
100 g (125 ml) sugar
60 ml water
12,5 ml lemon juice

TOPPING
125 g dark cooking chocolate, melted

Sift flour, salt and bicarbonate of soda into a bowl. Add brown sugar. Melt butter over medium heat, add milk and egg off the heat, beat well. Add to dry ingredients. Cover and chill one hour.

Filling
Place all ingredients in a saucepan. Stir over low heat until dates are soft. Allow to cool slightly.

Knead dough lightly on a floured surface. Roll out into a rectangle 350 mm by 200 mm. Cut in half, giving two 175 mm by 200 mm pieces. Cut one half into four by 50 mm strips. Spread date filling over three of the strips, place on top of each other, cover with the fourth strip. Repeat with other half of dough. Chill one hour.

Cut into 6 mm-thick slices, place on greased baking trays. Bake at 160 °C, 12 to 15 minutes. Remove to wire cooling racks. When biscuits are cool, drizzle with melted chocolate. Leave to set.

Makes about 30.

NOTE
To store biscuit dough, flavour it as you wish, wrap in clingwrap and store in refrigerator for up to two weeks or freeze for up to six months. Defrost 30 minutes before using.

NO-BAKE

CHOCOLATE FRIDGE ROLL

125 g butter *or* margarine, softened
250 g (300 ml) castor sugar
2 large eggs, beaten
75 g (190 ml) cocoa powder, sifted
100 g dark cooking chocolate, melted
12,5 ml kirsch liqueur *or* milk
300 g marie biscuits, roughly broken

Cream together butter and castor sugar until pale and fluffy. Add eggs, beat well. Add cocoa, melted chocolate and kirsch, whisk thoroughly. Form mixture into a roll about 75 mm in diameter. Wrap tightly in wax-paper and foil, refrigerate overnight.

Serve cut into thick slices.

Makes 10 to 12 slices.

CRISPY DIAGONALS

100 g marshmallows
225 g can full cream sweetened condensed milk
125 g butter *or* margarine
80 g (500 ml) Rice Krispies

TOPPING
150 g dark cooking chocolate, melted

Melt marshmallows, condensed milk and butter in a saucepan over low heat, stirring constantly. Stir in Rice Krispies, mix well. Press mixture into greased and lined 210 mm by 180 mm baking-tray. Chill in refrigerator until set.

Spread melted chocolate over surface, mark with a fork. Leave to set. Cut into diamond shapes and store in sealed container in refrigerator. Can also be frozen.

Makes 25.

NO-BAKE OAT BISCUITS

100 g marshmallows
100 g (100 ml) peanut butter
95 g (60 ml) honey
45 g butter *or* margarine
135 g (375 ml) rolled oats
150 g (250 ml) raisins
30 g (100 ml) desiccated coconut to coat

Place marshmallows, peanut butter, honey and butter in a saucepan, melt slowly over low heat, stir in oats and raisins. Spoon mixture into a greased and lined 220 mm-square pan, spread evenly. Leave in refrigerator overnight until set.

Cut into squares and toss each in coconut. Store in refrigerator.

Makes about 30 squares.

Crispy diagonals *(top)*; No-bake oat biscuits *(centre)*; Chocolate fridge roll *(bottom)*

CHOCOLATE CHERRY WEDGES

150 g packet white marshmallows
150 g chocolate
50 ml milk
100 g (155 ml) glacé cherries, chopped
65 g (150 ml) nuts, chopped (optional)
200 g packet marie biscuits, roughly broken

Combine marshmallows, chocolate and milk in a saucepan, melt over low heat. Remove from heat, stir in cherries, nuts and biscuits until combined. Spoon into 200 mm-diameter round glass pie plate. Press down with wooden spoon. Refrigerate until firm, cut into wedges.

Makes 16 wedges.

PECAN CARAMEL CHICKENS

100 g butter *or* margarine
200 g packet tennis biscuits, crushed
30 g (37,5 ml) castor sugar
12,5 ml caramel essence
25 ml natural yoghurt
100 g (250 ml) pecan nuts, chopped
100 g white chocolate, melted

Melt butter in a saucepan, add biscuits, castor sugar, caramel essence, yoghurt and pecan nuts, mix well. Spoon mixture into a 180 mm-square pan. Using back of a glass, press down firmly. Refrigerate two hours. Cut into bars or chicken shapes. Roll excess mixture into egg shapes. Fill piping bag with chocolate, decorate chickens and eggs.

Makes 18 bars or 14 chickens.

DATE AND BISCUIT SQUARES

250 g butter *or* margarine
200 g (250 ml) sugar
500 g stoned dates, chopped
4 g (10 ml) cocoa powder
2 eggs, lightly beaten
5 ml vanilla essence
4 x 200 g packets marie biscuits, roughly broken
30 g (37,5 ml) castor sugar

Melt butter, sugar and dates in a large saucepan, stir until mixture is soft and smooth. Stir in cocoa powder, cool slightly. Add eggs and vanilla essence, stir over low heat, do not allow to boil. Remove from heat, add biscuits, stir until well-combined. Pack mixture firmly into a greased 430 mm by 300 mm baking tray. Place a piece of greaseproof paper over biscuits, roll with rolling-pin until flat and compressed. Place in refrigerator to set.

Cut into squares, dust with castor sugar. Store in airtight container.

Makes 63 squares.

JAM BISCUITS

BAKEWELL BARS

400 g packet frozen shortcrust pastry, thawed *or*
   250 g home-made shortcrust pastry
100 g (75 ml) raspberry jam

FILLING
125 g butter *or* margarine, softened
125 g (150 ml) castor sugar
2 eggs, beaten
5 ml almond essence
125 g (225 ml) self-raising flour, sifted

TOPPING
65 g (100 ml) glacé cherries, halved
thin glacé icing (about 250 g icing sugar)

Roll out pastry and use to line a lightly greased, deep-sided 330 mm by 240 mm swiss roll pan, trim. Prick well with a fork. Spread jam over pastry. Refrigerate.

Filling
Cream together butter and castor sugar until pale and fluffy, gradually beat in eggs. Add almond essence. Sift in flour, fold in.

Spread filling over pastry. Bake at 180 °C, 20 to 30 minutes or until golden brown.

Topping
Scatter cherries over top, coat with glacé icing. Return to oven 10 minutes to crisp icing. Mark into bars, leave to cool in pan. Cut through completely, remove to wire cooling racks to cool, taking care not to crack icing more than is necessary.

Makes 40 bars.

APRICOT RINGS

400 g (800 ml) flour
120 g (145 ml) castor sugar
1 ml salt
grated rind of one lemon
25 g (30 ml) golden brown sugar
3 ml vanilla essence
1 egg, beaten
25 ml dark rum
250 g butter *or* margarine, cut up
20 g (40 ml) icing sugar, sifted
225 g (170 ml) smooth apricot jam, warmed

Sift flour into a bowl, make a well in centre. Add castor sugar, salt, lemon rind, brown sugar, vanilla essence, egg and rum. Dot butter over flour, rub in with fingertips to form a soft dough. Wrap in clingwrap, refrigerate two hours.

Roll out dough on a lightly floured surface to 3 mm thickness. Using plain cutters, cut out an equal number of rings and rounds of equal size. Place rings on top of rounds, arrange on lightly greased baking trays and bake at 180 °C, 10 to 15 minutes. Remove to wire cooling racks to cool completely.

Sift icing sugar generously over biscuits, fill centres with warmed jam. Leave to cool before serving.

Makes 20 pairs.

STRAWBERRY AND CINNAMON SHORTIES

300 g (415 ml) soft brown sugar
1 egg, beaten
200 g (400 ml) flour, sifted
5 ml baking-powder
10 ml ground cinnamon
1 ml salt
125 g butter *or* margarine, melted

ICING
37,5 ml water
300 g (580 ml) icing sugar, sifted
50 g (37,5 ml) strawberry jam

Place brown sugar in a bowl, stir in egg, mix well. Sift together dry ingredients and fold into sugar mixture. Add butter to make a stiff dough.

Roll dough into a sausage-shape 25 mm in diameter. Roll in wax-paper, refrigerate two to three hours.

Cut dough into slices of 7 mm thickness, place on lightly greased baking trays, leaving room for spreading.

Bake at 180 °C, eight to 10 minutes. Remove to wire cooling racks to cool completely.

Icing
Add water to icing sugar, stir well.

Coat tops of biscuits with icing, leave to set. Spoon about 1 ml of jam into centre of each.

Makes about 38.

Apricot rings *(left)* Bakewell bars *(centre)*; Strawberry and cinnamon shorties *(right)*

ICED FANCIES

BASIC DOUGH
200 g (400 ml) flour, sifted
pinch of salt
125 g butter *or* margarine, cut up
50 g (60 ml) castor sugar
1 egg, beaten
5 ml almond essence

FILLING
200 g (150 ml) smooth apricot jam *or* strawberry jam

ICING AND DECORATION
pink, yellow and white glacé icing
nonpareilles
glacé cherries, quartered
melted chocolate
iced flowers
royal icing for piping

Sift flour and salt into a bowl. Rub in butter until mixture resembles fine breadcrumbs. Stir in castor sugar. Beat together egg and almond essence, work into mixture. Knead well until mixture forms a stiff dough. (Alternatively combine mixture in food processor.) Turn out dough on to generously floured surface, roll out to 4 mm thickness.

Using different shaped cookie cutters, cut out a variety of biscuits. Place on lightly greased and lined baking trays.

Bake at 180°C, 15 to 18 minutes. Cool on wire cooling racks.

Spread half the biscuits with jam, top with remaining biscuits. Decorate as desired with icing, cherries and so on.

Makes 50 to 60 single biscuits, or 25 to 30 pairs.

THUMB COOKIES

120 g butter *or* margarine, softened
140 g (200 ml) soft brown sugar
100 g (125 ml) sugar
2 eggs, beaten
3 ml almond essence
400 g (800 ml) flour, sifted
2 ml baking-powder
about 105 g (80 ml) strawberry jam

Cream together butter and sugars until light and fluffy. Add beaten eggs, beat well. Stir in almond essence. Sift together flour and baking-powder, beat into mixture to form a soft dough. Wrap in clingwrap, chill in refrigerator 30 minutes.

Roll dough into walnut-sized balls. Place on lightly greased baking trays. Indent centre of each ball with thumb. Fill hollow with jam.

Bake at 180 °C, eight to 10 minutes. Remove from tray, leave to cool on wire cooling rack.

Makes about 50 cookies.

APRICOT PASTRY PRETZELS

400 g packet frozen puff pastry, thawed
400 g packet frozen shortcrust pastry, thawed
1 egg-yolk, beaten
175 g (135 ml) smooth apricot jam, warmed

Roll out pastries on lightly floured surface, each to measure 500 mm by 350 mm. Brush shortcrust pastry with egg-yolk, lay puff pastry on top, press gently together.

Cut into 15 mm-wide strips and twist into spirals, stretching slightly, so that puff pastry is on the outside. Form into pretzel shapes, secure ends using a little water.

Arrange on wetted baking trays, refrigerate 30 minutes.

Bake at 220 °C, about 15 minutes, or until crisp. Remove from oven, brush with jam. Remove to wire cooling racks to cool completely. Best eaten the same day.

Makes about 30.

Cream together butter and castor sugar until light and fluffy, add eggs and beat thoroughly. Stir in almonds, cinnamon, cream and a little flour until well mixed. Sift in remaining flour. Wrap dough in foil, refrigerate one hour.

Heat oil for frying. Roll out dough thinly on floured surface, cut out 50 mm fluted circles. Cut notches into every second flute. Brush centre with egg-white and lay three rounds one on top of the other to form a rosette. Using handle of wooden spoon make well in centre.

Place rosettes two or three at a time in hot oil, fry five minutes, until golden brown, turning once. Drain on absorbent kitchen paper towel. Allow to cool. Dust with sifted icing sugar. Fill centres with raspberry jam. Serve at once.

Makes 16 to 20.

ORANGE BRANDY CREAMS

125 g butter *or* margarine, softened
30 g (37,5 ml) castor sugar
1 egg-yolk
5 ml finely grated orange rind
115 g (330 ml) flour, sifted

BRANDY CREAM FILLING
125 g butter *or* margarine, softened
65 g (125 ml) icing sugar, sifted
3 ml vanilla essence
220 g (170 ml) smooth apricot jam
10 ml brandy
sifted icing sugar, extra

Cream together butter and castor sugar well. Beat in egg-yolk and orange rind, fold in sifted flour until a firm dough forms. Wrap in clingwrap, chill one hour.

Turn out on to a lightly floured surface, knead until smooth. Roll out to 3 mm thickness. Cut into 50 mm rounds using fluted pastry cutter. Cut out circle from centre of half the rounds with small fluted cutter.

Place rounds and rings on greased baking trays and bake at 160 °C, 15 to 20 minutes, until pale golden brown. Cool on wire cooling racks.

Brandy cream filling
Beat butter until soft and fluffy. Sift in icing sugar, beat well. Add vanilla essence. Place in piping bag fitted with a small star nozzle. Pipe a circle of butter cream around edge of round biscuits.

Sieve apricot jam, stir in brandy. Spoon a little jam into centre of butter cream. Top with ring biscuits. Dust with extra sifted icing sugar.

Makes about 18.

DEEP-FRIED RASPBERRY ROSETTES

150 g butter *or* margarine, softened
100 g (120 ml) castor sugar
2 eggs, beaten
50 g (100 ml) ground almonds
5 ml ground cinnamon
125 ml sour cream
500 g (4 x 250 ml) flour, sifted
oil for deep-frying
1 egg-white, lightly beaten
sifted icing sugar
200 g (150 ml) raspberry jam

DRIED FRUIT BISCUITS

FRUIT-CAKE BARS

150 g (250 ml) seedless raisins
150 g (250 ml) stoned dates, chopped
150 g (250 ml) candied peel, finely chopped
60 ml brandy
4 eggs, beaten
210 g (250 ml) castor sugar
5 ml vanilla essence
5 ml finely grated orange rind
2 ml salt
90 g (180 ml) flour, sifted
5 ml ground cinnamon
5 ml ground mixed spice
100 g (250 ml) walnuts, finely chopped

Place raisins, dates, peel and brandy in a small bowl. Cover and leave to macerate 24 hours.

Beat together eggs and castor sugar until pale and thick. Add vanilla essence, orange rind and salt, beat well.

Fold in flour, macerated fruit, spices and walnuts. Spread evenly over base of greased and lined 330 mm by 230 mm swiss roll pan.

Bake at 180 °C, 30 to 35 minutes. Allow to cool in pan before cutting into bars.

Makes about 40 bars.

DATE CHEWS

1 large egg, beaten
25 g (30 ml) castor sugar
1 ml salt
15 g butter *or* margarine, melted
250 g (415 ml) stoned dates, chopped
30 g (75 ml) walnuts, chopped
90 g (150 ml) self-raising flour, sifted
10 ml hot water
castor sugar for dredging

Beat together egg, castor sugar, salt and butter. Stir in dates and nuts. Add flour alternately with water, beat well.

Spread mixture into a greased and lined 185 mm-square cake pan and bake at 180 °C, 30 minutes.

Turn out on to wire cooling rack, dredge with castor sugar while warm. Leave to cool completely before cutting into squares.

Makes 16 squares.

MARZIPAN FANCIES

180 g butter *or* margarine, softened
80 g (90 ml) castor sugar
60 g almond paste (marzipan)
2 egg-yolks, beaten
10 ml brandy
15 g (25 ml) candied peel, finely chopped
225 g (450 ml) flour, sifted

TO DECORATE
halved glacé cherries
halved walnuts
hazel-nuts
chopped candied peel

Cream together butter and castor sugar until pale and fluffy. Mix together almond paste and egg-yolks, beat with a fork, add brandy, mix well. Gradually add to butter mixture, beating continuously.

Add candied peel. Sift in flour, mix well to form a firm dough. Break off walnut-sized pieces, form into balls with hands, place on lightly greased baking trays. Flatten slightly with a fork. Decorate with cherries, nuts or candied peel.

Bake at 180 °C, 10 minutes. Remove to wire cooling racks to cool.

Makes 25 to 30 biscuits.

Marzipan fancies *(left)*; Fruit-cake bars *(right)*

STEP-BY-STEP FLORENTINES

120 g (150 ml) sugar
125 ml fresh cream
40 g butter *or* margarine
200 g (335 ml) blanched almonds, finely chopped
40 g (60 ml) glacé cherries, chopped
140 g (180 ml) special moist cake fruit mixture (in box or jar)
50 g (100 ml) flour, sifted

TOPPING
250 g dark chocolate, melted

1 Combine sugar, cream and butter in heavy-bottomed saucepan, dissolve slowly, bring to the boil. Remove from heat, stir in remaining ingredients.

2 Drop 5 ml amounts of mixture on to greased baking trays, leaving plenty of room between each to allow for spreading. Flatten slightly with wetted fork.

3 Bake biscuits at 180°C, five minutes. Remove from oven and, using a 50 mm scone cutter, pull in edges of each biscuit. Return to oven a further five to 10 minutes, or until golden brown. Cool briefly on baking trays before carefully removing to cooling rack to cool completely.

4 Evenly spread underside of each biscuit with melted chocolate.

5 When partially set, mark wavy lines on chocolate with a cake-decorating comb, or fork. Leave to dry.

Makes 32 biscuits.

Raisin walnut cookies *(left)*; Fruit and nut rounds *(right)*

RAISIN WALNUT COOKIES

100 g butter *or* margarine, softened
100 g (137,5 ml) soft brown sugar
225 g (450 ml) flour, sifted
3 ml bicarbonate of soda
1 egg, beaten
5 ml vanilla essence
75 g (125 ml) seedless raisins, finely chopped
50 g (125 ml) walnuts, finely chopped

Cream together butter and brown sugar. Sift flour and bicarbonate of soda into a bowl. Add to creamed mixture, together with egg, vanilla essence, raisins and walnuts, mix well.

Break off pieces of dough the size of a walnut, form into a ball, place on lightly greased baking trays, press down lightly with fingertips.

Bake at 190 °C, 12 minutes or until pale golden brown. Remove to wire cooling racks to cool completely. Store in airtight tin.

Makes about 45.

FRUIT AND NUT ROUNDS

200 g butter *or* margarine, softened
135 g (160 ml) castor sugar
250 g (500 ml) flour, sifted
2 ml salt
50 g (90 ml) seedless raisins, finely chopped
30 g (50 ml) glacé cherries, finely chopped
80 g (200 ml) walnuts, finely chopped
4 g (5 ml) candied peel, finely chopped

Cream together butter and castor sugar until light and fluffy. Add remaining ingredients, mix well to form a dough.

Form into a sausage shape about 250 mm long on sheet of greaseproof paper. Wrap tightly into a roll, refrigerate one hour until firm.

Cut into 7 mm-thick slices, place on lightly greased baking trays.

Bake at 180 °C, about 20 minutes, until pale golden brown. Leave to cool five minutes on trays before removing to wire cooling racks to cool completely.

Makes about 25.

PIPED AND PRESSED

PIPED BISCUITS

BASIC MIXTURE
125 g (250 ml) flour, sifted
6 g (12,5 ml) custard powder
30 g (37,5 ml) castor sugar
90 g butter *or* margarine, softened
about 100 ml milk

1 Sift dry ingredients into an electric mixer-bowl. Beat well, adding milk gradually until mixture is soft and creamy.

This mixture makes about 15 biscuits.

2 Remove one-third quantity basic mixture, set aside. Add rind and colouring to remainder.

Orange stars
**one quantity basic mixture
5 ml finely grated orange rind
orange food colouring
sifted icing sugar**

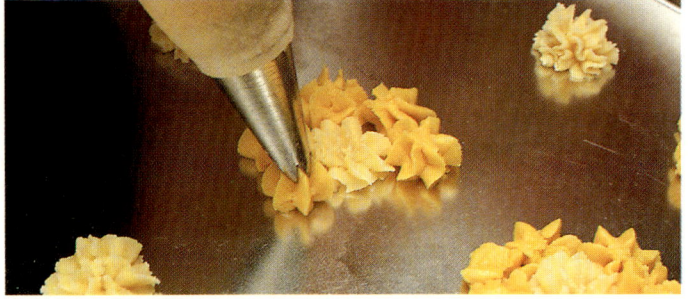

3 Fill piping bag fitted with a medium star nozzle, with basic mixture. Pipe stars, spaced well apart on to a lightly greased baking tray. Fill piping bag with orange mixture and pipe a circle of stars around those on tray.

Bake at 180°C, about 20 minutes. Dust with sifted icing sugar.

Crunchy lemon drops
**one quantity basic mixture
5 ml finely grated lemon rind
50 g (62,5 ml) colour sugar crystals**

5 Add lemon rind to basic mixture, work in well. Place in piping bag fitted with a medium, open star nozzle. Pipe 50 mm-diameter rounds on to a lightly greased baking tray. Sprinkle with sugar crystals. Bake at 180°C, 15 to 20 minutes.

Cherry shells
**one quantity basic mixture
glacé cherries, cut into quarters**

4 Fill piping bag fitted with a large star nozzle, with basic mixture. Pipe shells on to a lightly greased baking tray. Place cherry pieces on points. Bake at 180°C, about 20 minutes.

Viennese fingers
**one quantity basic mixture
90 g cooking chocolate, melted**

6 Fill piping bag fitted with a medium, open star nozzle, with basic mixture. Pipe 'S' shapes on to a lightly greased baking tray. Bake at 180°C, 15 minutes. Remove to wire cooling racks to cool completely.

Spoon melted chocolate into greaseproof paper piping bag. Snip off tip, drizzle a zigzag pattern over each biscuit. Leave to dry.

Chocolate shorties
**one quantity basic mixture
50 g cooking chocolate, melted**

7 Fill piping bag fitted with a medium, open star nozzle, with basic mixture. Pipe 75 mm fingers on to a lightly greased baking tray. Bake at 180°C, 15 to 20 minutes. Cool on wire cooling rack. Dip both ends of each biscuit into melted chocolate. Leave to dry on wax-paper.

From left to right: Melting orange creams; Cherry shells; Chocolate melts

PIPED DELIGHTS

BASIC DOUGH
250 g butter *or* margarine, softened
40 g (80 ml) icing sugar, sifted
190 g (375 ml) flour, sifted
60 g (125 ml) cornflour, sifted

Cream together butter and icing sugar until pale and fluffy. Stir flour and cornflour into creamed mixture, mix to form a firm but pliable dough.

MELTING ORANGE CREAMS
one quantity basic dough

ORANGE CREAM FILLING
60 g butter *or* margarine, softened
130 g (250 ml) icing sugar, sifted
5 ml finely grated orange rind
12,5 ml freshly squeezed orange juice

TO DECORATE
sifted icing sugar

Spoon dough into a piping bag fitted with a large, open rose nozzle. Pipe large stars on to lightly greased baking trays. Bake at 180°C, 12 to 15 minutes. Cool on wire cooling rack.

Orange cream filling
Cream butter, beat in icing sugar and orange rind. Gradually beat in orange juice.

Sandwich pairs of biscuits together with filling. Dust lightly with icing sugar.

Makes about 22 pairs.

CHOCOLATE MELTS
one quantity basic dough
100 g dark chocolate, melted

Spoon dough into a piping bag fitted with a medium, open rose nozzle. Pipe 'S' shapes, circles and fingers on to lightly greased baking trays.

Bake at 180°C, 15 minutes. Cool. Remove to wire cooling rack to cool completely. Dip ends of biscuits in melted chocolate, leave on wax-paper to dry.

Makes 35 to 40.

CHERRY SHELLS
one quantity basic dough
glacé cherries, cut into quarters
warmed, sieved apricot jam

Spoon dough into a piping bag fitted with a large, open star nozzle. Pipe shells on to lightly greased baking trays, place cherry pieces on points.

Bake at 180°C, about 15 minutes. Cool on wire cooling rack. Carefully brush warmed jam over surface of each biscuit.

Makes about 40.

PIPED VANILLA ROSETTES

375 g butter *or* margarine, softened
60 g (120 ml) icing sugar, sifted
5 ml vanilla essence
270 g (540 ml) flour, sifted
90 g (180 ml) cornflour, sifted

Cream together butter, icing sugar and vanilla essence. Sift in flour and cornflour, beat well until combined.

Place dough in a piping bag fitted with a large, open star nozzle. Pipe rosettes on to a lightly greased baking tray

Bake at 180°C, 10 to 15 minutes, or until pale golden brown. Remove to wire cooling rack to cool.

Makes about 55 single biscuits.

Biscuits may be sandwiched together with melted chocolate, if desired.

PIPED CHOCOLATE BISCUITS

300 g butter *or* margarine, softened
60 g (120 ml) icing sugar, sifted
200 g (360 ml) self-raising flour, sifted
50 g (100 ml) cornflour, sifted
40 g (100 ml) cocoa powder, sifted
5 ml vanilla essence
1 egg, lightly beaten

TO COMPLETE
vanilla butter icing
sifted icing sugar

Cream together butter and icing sugar until light and fluffy. Sift together dry ingredients. Add to creamed mixture, beat well. Mix in vanilla essence and egg.

Spoon biscuit dough into piping bag fitted with a star nozzle. Pipe flat rosettes on to lightly greased baking trays. Space well apart to allow for spreading.

Bake at 180°C, 10 to 12 minutes, or until firm. Cool slightly, remove carefully from baking trays. Leave to cool on wire cooling rack.

To complete
Sandwich biscuits together with a vanilla-flavoured butter icing, sift icing sugar over the top. Store in airtight tins.

Makes 34 to 36 single biscuits, or 17 to 18 pairs.

PRESSED COOKIES

250 g butter *or* margarine, softened
180 g (215 ml) castor sugar
2 eggs, beaten
5 ml almond essence
500 g (4 x 250 ml) flour, sifted
60 g (120 ml) cornflour, sifted
8 ml baking-powder

Cream together butter and castor sugar well. Gradually beat in eggs and almond essence.

Sift together flour, cornflour and baking-powder into a bowl, work into creamed mixture.

Turn out on to a lightly floured surface, knead lightly. Wrap in clingwrap, chill in refrigerator, 30 minutes.

Form a portion of the dough into a sausage-shape and place in biscuit machine. Use desired disc and press biscuits on to lightly greased baking trays.

Bake at 200 °C, 10 to 12 minutes, or until pale golden brown. Remove to wire cooling racks to cool completely.

VARIATION
Almond and chocolate cookies
Work 5 g (12, 5 ml) cocoa powder into one-quarter of the dough. Form into sausage shape. Wrap basic dough around the chocolate dough, place in cookie machine. Press out desired shape. Bake as above.

Leave biscuits plain, decorate with almond-flavoured glacé icing or sandwich together with an almond butter cream.

Makes about 140 biscuits.

GINGER AND SPICE

BUSY LIZZIES

225 g (375 ml) seedless raisins
60 ml orange juice
90 g (180 ml) flour, sifted
7 ml baking-powder
7 ml ground cinnamon
1 ml ground nutmeg
1 ml ground cloves
25 g butter *or* margarine, softened
50 g (60 ml) golden brown sugar
2 small eggs, beaten
200 g (500 ml) walnuts, roughly chopped
100 g (170 ml) candied peel, finely chopped
250 g (390 ml) glacé cherries, halved

Stir together raisins and orange juice, allow to stand one hour.

Sift together dry ingredients into a bowl. Cream together butter and brown sugar in a large mixer-bowl, add eggs, beat well. Stir in sifted dry ingredients. Add soaked raisins, walnuts, peel and cherries, mix well.

Drop 5 ml amounts of mixture about 25 mm apart on to lightly greased baking trays. With wet fingers, press fruit and nuts into dough to form a compact ball.

Bake at 160°C, about 15 minutes or until golden brown and firm. Remove to wire cooling racks to cool completely. Store in airtight tin.

Makes about 60.

SPICED OATMEAL DROPS

90 g butter *or* margarine
40 g (25 ml) liquid honey
190 g (375 ml) flour, sifted
3 ml ground cinnamon
3 ml ground cloves
3 ml grated nutmeg
3 ml salt
3 ml bicarbonate of soda
3 ml baking-powder
135 g (375 ml) rolled oats
180 g (250 ml) soft brown sugar
1 egg, beaten
125 ml evaporated milk *or* thin cream

Melt butter and honey, remove from heat.

Sift together next seven ingredients into a bowl, stir in oats and brown sugar.

Beat egg and evaporated milk into melted butter and honey mixture. Add to dry ingredients, mix well. Drop 10 ml amounts, far apart, on to lightly greased baking trays, bake at 180°C, 15 to 20 minutes until golden brown.

Remove from oven, cool on wire cooling racks. Store in airtight tins. Crisp up in a low oven, if necessary, just before serving.

Makes about 50.

CINNAMON BISCUITS

125 g butter *or* margarine, softened
100 g (125 ml) sugar
200 g (125 ml) liquid honey
1 extra-large egg, beaten
5 ml vanilla essence
310 g (625 ml) flour, sifted
10 ml ground cinnamon
1 ml grated nutmeg
1 ml salt
2 ml bicarbonate of soda
80 g (100 ml) sugar, mixed with
5 ml ground cinnamon

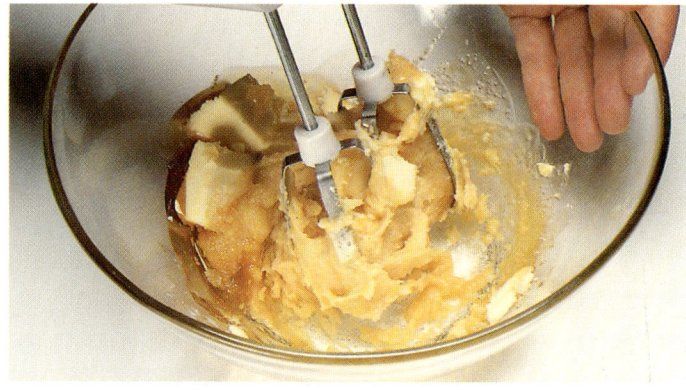

1 Cream together butter, sugar and honey until pale and fluffy.

2 Add egg and vanilla essence.

3 Sift together flour, spices, salt and bicarbonate of soda into a mixing bowl. Add to creamed mixture to form a soft dough.

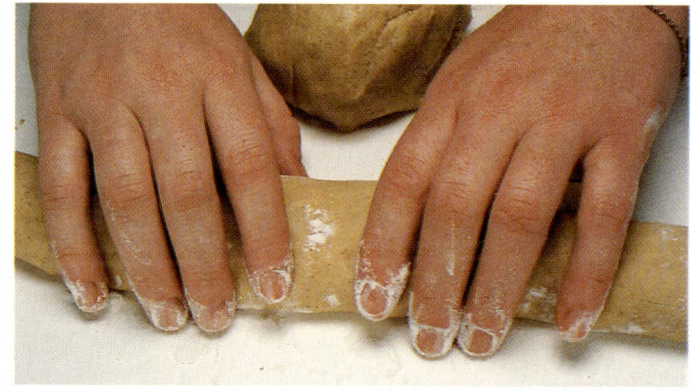

4 Turn out dough on to a lightly floured surface, knead gently. Working with one half at a time, roll dough into a sausage-shape about 60 mm in diameter. Wrap tightly in wax-paper, then in foil. Repeat with remaining dough. Chill rolls in refrigerator overnight.

5 Cut into 6 mm-thick slices.

6 Arrange slices, far apart, on lightly greased baking trays. Sprinkle with cinnamon sugar mixture, press down gently with the back of a teaspoon.

To complete
Bake at 190°C, 10 to 12 minutes. Remove to wire cooling racks to cool completely. Store in airtight containers.

Makes about 56.

ORANGE AND GINGER BISCUITS

60 g butter *or* **margarine, softened**
125 g (155 ml) sugar
5 ml finely grated orange rind
1 egg, beaten
15 ml milk
3 ml vanilla essence
75 g (135 ml) self-raising flour, sifted
150 g (300 ml) flour, sifted
12,5 ml ground ginger
sifted icing sugar to serve (optional)

Cream together butter, sugar and orange rind. Add egg, milk and vanilla essence, beat well. Sift together dry ingredients, beat into creamed mixture to form a firm dough.

Place in cookie-press and press out shapes on to lightly greased baking trays.

Bake at 180°C, 12 to 15 minutes or until pale golden brown. Remove to wire cooling rack to cool completely. Dust with sifted icing sugar if desired. Store in airtight container.

Makes about 40.

PRESSED GINGER BISCUITS

250 g butter *or* margarine, softened
2 eggs, beaten
400 g (500 ml) sugar
400 g (250 ml) golden syrup
700 g (1 400 ml) flour, sifted
10 ml bicarbonate of soda
10 ml ground ginger
10 ml ground cinnamon
10 ml ground mixed spice

GINGER ICING
200 g (400 ml) icing sugar, sifted
60 g butter *or* margarine
37,5 ml ginger syrup *or* 5 ml ground ginger mixed with 37,5ml golden syrup

Beat together butter, eggs, sugar and syrup until combined and creamy. Sift together dry ingredients, add to creamed mixture to form a soft dough.

Place dough in biscuit-maker, press out on to lightly greased baking trays.

Bake at 180 °C, 12 to 15 minutes. Remove to wire cooling rack. When cool, sandwich together with ginger icing.

Ginger icing
Melt all ingredients in a small saucepan, stir until combined. Cool completely, beat well.

Makes about 140 single biscuits or 70 pairs.

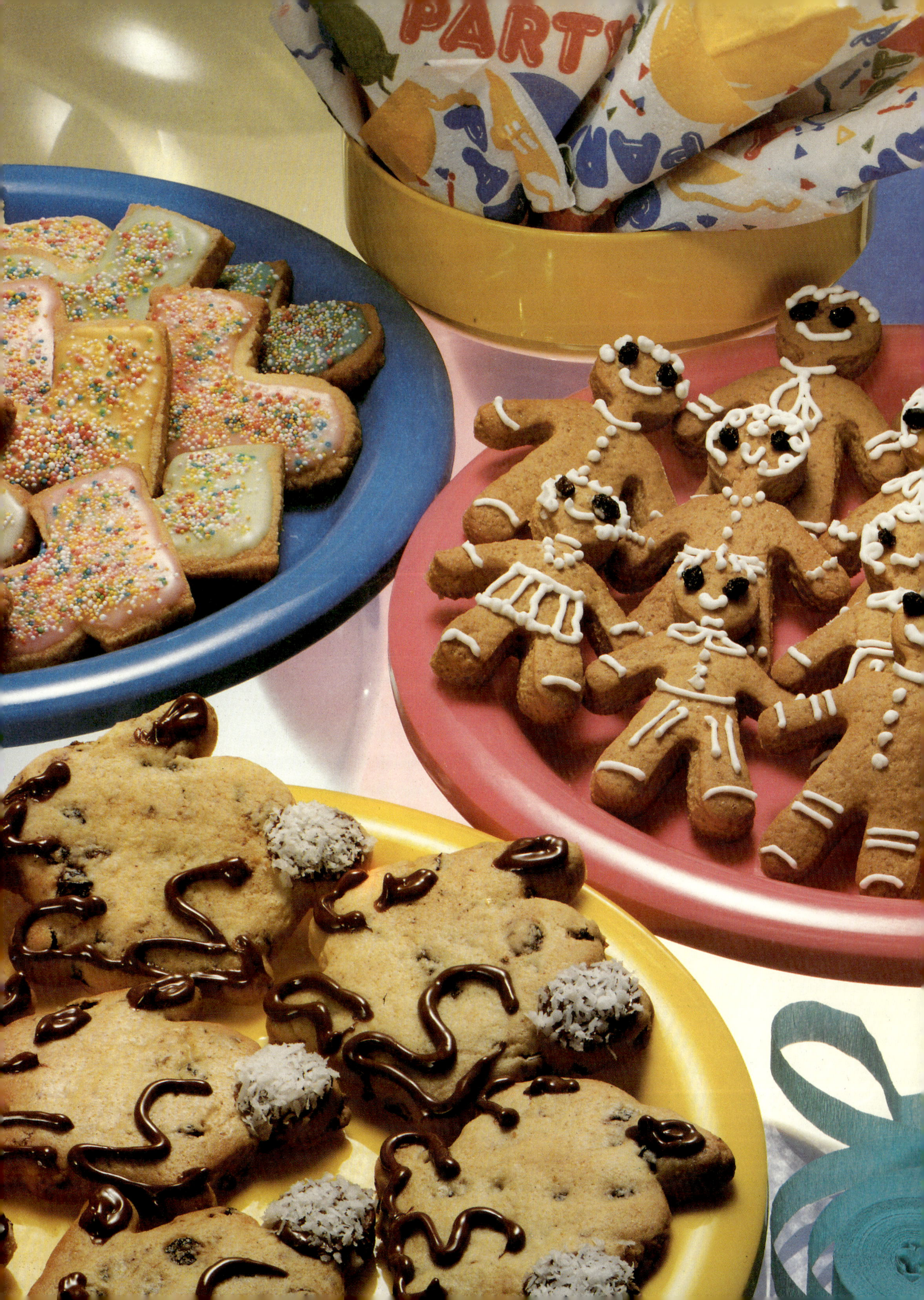
PARTY

KIDDIES' TREATS

GINGERBREAD BOYS AND GIRLS

250 g (500 ml) flour, sifted
5 ml baking-powder
7 ml ground ginger
3 ml bicarbonate of soda
90 g butter *or* margarine, softened
90 g (125 ml) soft brown sugar
110 g (70 ml) golden syrup
25 ml - 37,5 ml milk

TO DECORATE
currants
white royal icing

Sift together flour, baking-powder, ginger and bicarbonate of soda into a bowl. Cream together butter and brown sugar in food processor or electric mixer-bowl. Add syrup, mix well. Work in dry ingredients, adding enough milk to make a firm but pliable dough. Knead very thoroughly.

Wrap dough in wax-paper, refrigerate 30 minutes. Roll out between two sheets of greaseproof paper (or use Doughmaster plastic sheets) to 5 mm thickness. Cut out dough using suitable biscuit cutter or template given on page 85. Lift carefully on to lightly greased baking trays and press currants into dough for eyes. Carefully separate arms from body slightly to give a more definite outline.

Bake at 220 °C, about eight minutes, taking care not to scorch biscuits. Leave on trays one minute, then remove to wire cooling racks to cool completely.

Decorate boys and girls with royal icing, allow to set and serve at once. Store (without icing) in airtight tins. Crisp up in low oven if necessary.

Makes about 45.

RABBIT BISCUITS

90 g butter *or* margarine, softened
90 g (105 ml) castor sugar
1 egg, lightly beaten
finely grated rind of one orange
240 g (430 ml) self-raising flour, sifted
2 ml ground mixed spice
60 g (100 ml) currants
50 ml milk

TO DECORATE
150 g dark chocolate, melted
desiccated coconut

Cream together butter and castor sugar, beat in egg and orange rind. Sift in flour and spice, add currants. Beat well to make a soft, pliable dough. Knead quickly, roll out on a lightly floured surface to 5 mm thickness.

Cut out rabbit shapes using a suitable cutter or the template given on page 85. Place on lightly greased baking trays, bake at 180 °C, 10 minutes. (Refrigerate dough between rollings to firm up.) Brush biscuits with milk, return to oven and continue baking about 10 minutes or until golden brown and crisp. Cool on wire cooling rack.

To decorate
Coat ears, feet and bobtails with melted chocolate. Sprinkle tails with coconut while chocolate is still wet. Leave to dry on wax-paper. Store (without decoration) in airtight tins.

Makes 28 biscuits.

BOOT BISCUITS

125 g butter *or* margarine, softened
120 g (145 ml) castor sugar
1 egg, beaten
1 ml vanilla essence
250 g (500 ml) flour, sifted

GLACÉ ICING
little water to mix
100 g (190 ml) icing sugar, sifted

TO DECORATE
assorted liquid food colourings
***nonpareilles* (100s and 1 000s)**

Combine all ingredients in a food processor until a firm dough is formed. Knead one minute on a lightly floured surface. Roll out to 6 mm thickness. Using boot template given on page 85, cut out biscuits. Place on greased baking trays. Bake at 190 °C, 15 to 20 minutes or until pale golden brown. Remove to wire cooling rack to cool.

Glacé icing
Gradually add water to icing sugar until smooth consistency is formed and icing coats the back of a spoon. Divide icing into portions, colour each as desired.

Coat top of each biscuit almost to the edge with glacé icing. Sprinkle with *nonpareilles* while icing is still wet. Leave to dry.

Makes 44 biscuits.

Boot biscuits *(left)*; Gingerbread boys and girls *(right)*; Rabbit biscuits *(bottom)*

1 Cookie-press butter biscuits
2 Sparkling sugar stars
3 Crunchy biscuits
4 Marshmallow rings
5 Lollipop biscuits

SPARKLING SUGAR STARS

150 g (300 ml) flour, sifted
60 g (125 ml) semolina
125 g butter *or* margarine, softened
90 g (105 ml) castor sugar
1 egg, separated
10 ml milk

TO DECORATE
crushed cube sugar
coloured sugar crystals
caramel brown sugar

Combine flour and semolina, rub in butter. Add castor sugar. Beat together egg-yolk and milk, mix into dry ingredients to form a stiff dough. Wrap in waxwrap, refrigerate 15 minutes.

Roll out dough on floured surface to 5 mm thickness and using a star cutter, cut out biscuits. Brush each with lightly beaten egg-white, sprinkle with crushed cube sugar, coloured crystals or caramel brown sugar.

Bake at 180°C, 12 to 15 minutes until pale golden. Cool slightly before removing to wire cooling racks to cool completely.

Makes 36 to 40 biscuits.

COOKIE-PRESS BUTTER BISCUITS

425 g butter *or* margarine, softened
180 g (215 ml) castor sugar
630 g (1 260 ml) flour, sifted
1 egg, beaten
grated rind of one lemon
30 g (75 ml) cocoa powder, sifted
10 ml vanilla essence

Cream together butter and castor sugar until light and fluffy. Sift in flour, beat in egg. Mixture should form a stiff dough. Divide into three.

Work lemon rind into one-third, cocoa into second and vanilla essence into third. Wrap each in waxwrap, chill in refrigerator 15 minutes.

Using separately or combined, push flavoured biscuit mixture through cookie-press on to greased baking trays, making a wide variety of shapes.

Bake at 190°C, eight to 10 minutes until pale golden brown. Leave to cool on trays a few minutes, remove to wire cooling racks to cool completely.

Makes about 190 biscuits.

CRUNCHY BISCUITS

120 g butter *or* margarine, softened
65 g (80 ml) castor sugar
1 egg, beaten
140 g (250 ml) self-raising flour, sifted
90 g (150 ml) seedless raisins
100 g (500 ml) lightly crushed cornflakes

Cream together butter and castor sugar until light and fluffy. Add egg and beat well. Sift in flour, add raisins and 50 g (250 ml) cornflakes. Drop spoonfuls into remaining cornflakes, roll lightly to coat and place on well greased baking trays. Flatten lightly with the back of a fork, bake at 180°C, about 20 minutes.

Makes 24.

MARSHMALLOW RINGS

BASE
60 g butter *or* margarine, softened
90 g (125 ml) soft brown sugar
1 egg, lightly beaten
5 ml vanilla essence
150 g (300 ml) wholewheat flour, sifted and husks replaced

TOPPING
200 g (250 ml) sugar
250 ml water
10 g (15 ml) gelatine
5 ml vanilla essence
80 g (250 ml) desiccated coconut, toasted
265 g (200 ml) jam, heated

Base
Cream together butter and brown sugar, beat in egg and vanilla essence. Add flour and mix to form a firm dough. Roll out on lightly floured surface to 5 mm thickness. Using a 50 mm-diameter round cutter, cut out biscuits and place on lightly greased baking trays. Bake at 180°C, about 10 minutes. Leave to cool on trays.

Topping
Combine sugar and water in small saucepan, sprinkle gelatine over surface. When sugar has dissolved, bring to the boil, reduce heat, simmer about five minutes. Remove from heat, leave to cool.

Pour syrup with vanilla essence into bowl of electric mixer, beat on high speed about 15 minutes until mixture becomes thick and white. Spoon into piping bag fitted with a 10 mm plain nozzle.

Pipe marshmallow in a circle around edge of biscuit base. Dip top of biscuit in toasted coconut and spoon 5 ml jam into centre. Place in refrigerator to set before serving.

Makes about 20 biscuits.

LOLLIPOP BISCUITS

100 g butter *or* margarine, softened
105 g (125 ml) castor sugar
2 eggs, beaten
finely grated rind of half a lemon
225 g (450 ml) flour, sifted
18 wooden lollipop sticks

TO DECORATE
royal icing
various colour pastes
Smarties

Cream together butter and castor sugar until light and fluffy. Beat in eggs and lemon rind. Sift in flour, mix well until mixture forms a firm dough. Turn out and knead lightly on floured surface.

1 Roll out dough to 5 mm thickness.

2 Cut out biscuits using a 40 mm-diameter plain round cutter.

3 Place biscuits on lightly greased baking trays. Press in sticks.

To complete
Bake at 180°C, 15 to 20 minutes until golden brown. Cool a few minutes on trays before removing to wire cooling racks to cool completely. When cold, ice a variety of faces on to biscuits using royal icing and Smarties. Leave to set.

Makes 18 lollipops.

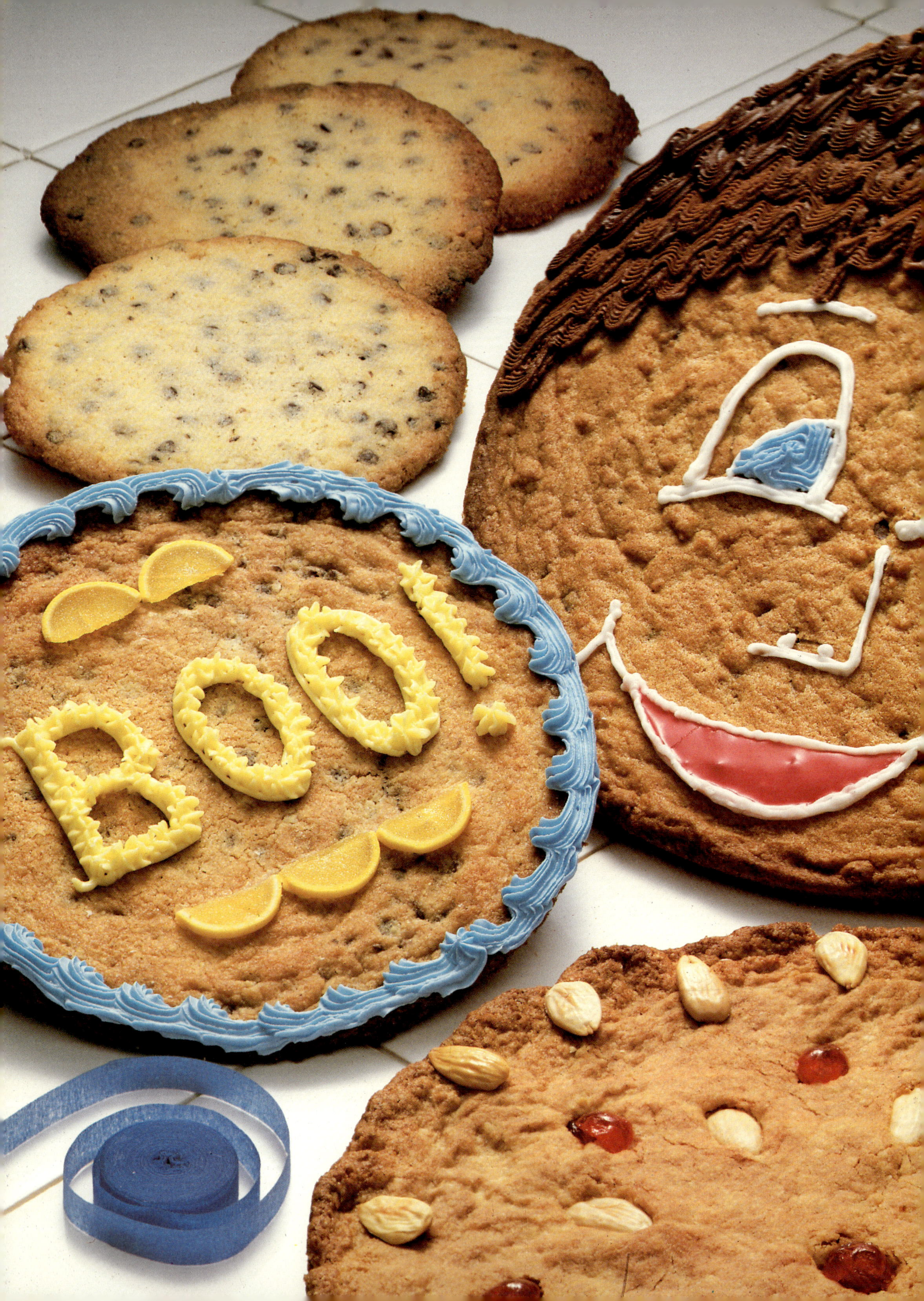
Boo!

CHOC-CHIP MONSTER COOKIES

190 g butter *or* margarine, softened
150 g (190 ml) sugar
1 egg-white
5 ml vanilla essence
95 g (190 ml) flour, sifted
pinch of salt
100 g chocolate chips
75 g (125 ml) blanched almonds, chopped

Cream together butter and sugar until light and fluffy. Add egg-white and vanilla essence. Sift together flour and salt, stir into creamed mixture. Add chocolate chips and almonds, mix well.

Form dough into large balls and place on greased and lined baking trays. Flatten each ball with a fork, bake at 180 °C, about 10 minutes. Leave to cool. Remove to wire cooling racks.

Makes about 10 by 120 mm-diameter cookies.

ICED GIANT COOKIES

250 g butter *or* margarine, softened
180 g (250 ml) caramel brown sugar
100 g (125 ml) sugar
2 eggs, beaten
280 g (560 ml) flour, sifted
5 ml bicarbonate of soda
pinch of salt
5 ml vanilla essence
100 g chocolate chips
100 g (250 ml) walnuts, chopped

ROYAL ICING
1 large egg-white
200 g (385 ml) icing sugar, sifted
little lemon juice, strained
variety of colour pastes

Cream together butter and sugars until light and fluffy. Gradually beat in eggs and continue beating until well blended. Sift together flour, bicarbonate of soda and salt, add to creamed mixture. Stir in vanilla essence, chocolate chips and walnuts. Divide mixture into three.

Line baking trays with greaseproof paper, grease lightly. Draw three by 250 mm-diameter circles on to paper and spread mixture inside circle lines.

Bake at 180 °C, about 12 minutes until lightly browned. Leave to cool on wire cooling racks. Remove from baking trays, peel off paper.

Royal icing
Break egg-white into clean, grease-free bowl. Whip lightly. Gradually add icing sugar, beating continuously to give a stiff consistency. Add lemon juice. Beat about five minutes until icing resembles well-beaten cream and stands in stiff, glossy peaks. Store in airtight container and keep covered at all times. Beat well before using and keep covered with damp cloth while using.

Colour royal icing with various colour pastes, ice face, 'Boo' etc on cooled cookies. Leave to set.

Makes three by 250 mm-diameter giant cookies.

SUPER OATMEAL COOKIE

95 g (190 ml) flour, sifted
90 g (190 ml) rolled oats
3 ml baking-powder
2 ml bicarbonate of soda
80 g butter *or* margarine, softened
60 g (80 ml) soft brown sugar
65 g (80 ml) sugar
1 egg, beaten
5 ml vanilla essence

TO DECORATE
whole blanched almonds
10 - 12 glacé cherries, halved

Combine flour, oats, baking-powder and bicarbonate of soda in a large mixing bowl. Cream together butter and sugars until pale and fluffy. Add egg and vanilla essence. Beat in flour mixture to form a stiff dough.

Press dough evenly into a lightly greased 300 mm-diameter round baking pan. Decorate attractively with almonds and cherries.

Bake at 180 °C, 12 to 15 minutes until golden brown. Remove from oven and place on wire cooling rack to cool completely before removing from pan.

Serves 10.

Choc-chip monster cookies *(left)*; Iced giant cookies *(centre and right)*; Super oatmeal cookie *(bottom)*

CITRUS BISCUITS

NUTTY LEMON SLICES

BASE
90 g butter *or* margarine, softened
20 g (25 ml) castor sugar
95 g (190 ml) flour, sifted
40 g (80 ml) cornflour, sifted

FILLING
397 g can full cream sweetened condensed milk
2 egg-yolks, beaten
finely grated rind of one lemon
125 ml lemon juice

TOPPING
2 egg-whites
50 g (60 ml) castor sugar
40 g (125 ml) desiccated coconut
50 g (125 ml) flaked almonds

1 Base Cream together butter and castor sugar until light and fluffy. Sift together dry ingredients, add gradually to creamed mixture, beat well to form a firm dough. Turn out on to a floured surface, knead five minutes.

2 Press evenly over base of a deep, greased and base-lined 160 mm by 260 mm baking pan. Bake at 180°C, 15 minutes or until lightly browned. Allow to cool.

3 Filling Combine condensed milk, egg-yolks, lemon rind and juice in a mixing bowl, mix well. Pour over base, bake at 180°C, 10 minutes until set.

4 Topping Beat egg-whites until soft peaks form, gradually add castor sugar, beat until sugar dissolves. Fold in coconut.

To complete
Spread topping over filling, sprinkle with flaked almonds. Bake at 180°C, 15 minutes until golden brown. Leave to cool in pan before cutting into bars or squares.

Makes 14 bars or 21 squares.

CREAMY LEMON DREAMS

BASE
150 g butter *or* margarine, softened
100 g (120 ml) castor sugar
grated rind of one lemon
1 large egg, beaten
250 g (500 ml) flour, sifted

FILLING
4 large eggs, beaten
145 g (180 ml) sugar
125 ml freshly squeezed lemon juice
12,5 ml cornflour
25 ml water

TOPPING
100 g butter *or* margarine, softened
200 g (400 ml) flour, sifted
50 g (62,5 ml) castor sugar
50 g (100 ml) ground almonds

TO COMPLETE
sifted icing sugar

1 Base Cream together butter, castor sugar and lemon rind until light and creamy, beat in egg. Gradually work in flour until mixture forms a firm dough.

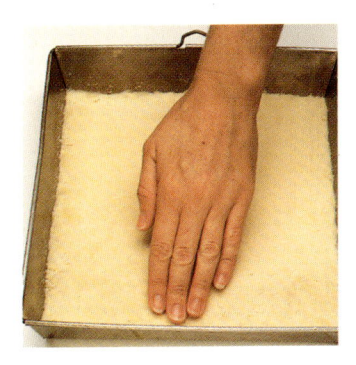

2 Press dough into a deep greased 200 mm-square cake pan. Bake at 180°C, 12 to 15 minutes or until golden brown.

3 Filling Whisk together eggs and sugar until pale and thick. Gradually beat in lemon juice. Pour into a saucepan. Mix cornflour with water, add to mixture. Stir over heat until mixture boils and thickens.

4 Spoon filling evenly into baked crust.

5 Topping Rub butter into flour until mixture resembles coarse breadcrumbs. Stir in castor sugar and almonds. Sprinkle over filling.

6 Bake at 180°C, 15 minutes or until topping is golden brown. Remove from oven and leave in pan to cool. Sift icing sugar over the top.

To complete
Cut into bars, remove from pan and place on wire cooling rack to cool completely.

Makes 20 bars.

CHOCOLATE WHEELS WITH NUTS

250 g (500 ml) flour, sifted
60 g (75 ml) sugar
grated rind of one lemon
200 g butter *or* margarine, chilled and diced
5 ml lemon juice
2 ml caramel essence
150 g chocolate, melted
30 g (50 ml) nibbed almonds

Place flour, sugar and lemon rind in food processor, blend in butter, lemon juice and essence until a soft dough is formed. Form into a ball, wrap and refrigerate one hour.

Roll out on a lightly floured surface to 6 mm thickness, cut into rounds with biscuit cutter. Cut out centres to form rings.

Place on lightly greased baking trays, bake at 160°C, 10 to 12 minutes or until lightly browned. When cool, dip half of each biscuit into melted chocolate, sprinkle with a few nuts.

Makes 30 to 35 biscuits.

47

VANILLA ROUNDS

100 g butter *or* **margarine, softened**
175 g (220 ml) sugar
1 extra-large egg, lightly beaten
5 ml vanilla essence
3 ml finely grated lemon rind
175 g (350 ml) flour, sifted
1 ml salt
10 ml baking-powder

TO COMPLETE
sugar
chopped nuts

Cream together butter and sugar until light and fluffy. Add egg, beat well. Mix in vanilla essence and lemon rind. Sift together flour, salt and baking-powder, add to creamed mixture to form a firm dough.

Chill in refrigerator, one hour. Divide dough in half, form into two rolls, each about 50 mm in diameter. Wrap tightly in wax-paper, then in foil. Chill until firm. (May be frozen at this stage.)

Cut rolls into 5 mm-thick slices. Sprinkle with sugar or chopped nuts, or leave plain. Place on greased baking trays and bake at 200°C, 10 minutes. Place on wire cooling rack to cool. Store in airtight tin.

Makes 30.

CHOCOLATE DIP BISCUITS

180 g butter *or* **margarine, softened**
180 g (215 ml) castor sugar
1 large egg, beaten
10 ml finely grated orange rind
375 g (750 ml) flour, sifted
10 ml baking-powder
5 ml salt

TO COAT
100 g plain chocolate
25 ml water
5 ml oil
30 g (37,5 ml) castor sugar

Cream together butter and castor sugar until light and fluffy. Beat in egg and orange rind. Sift flour, baking-powder and salt into creamed mixture. Stir until well combined. Cover and chill in refrigerator, one hour.

Roll out dough on a floured surface to 3 mm thickness. Cut into assorted shapes using floured biscuit cutters. Arrange on lightly greased baking trays. Bake at 190°C, 10 minutes. Remove to wire cooling racks, leave to cool completely.

Break chocolate into small pieces, place in a saucepan with water, oil and castor sugar. Stir over low heat until smooth, cool slightly.

Dip half of each biscuit into chocolate. Leave to set on wax-paper. Store in airtight containers.

Makes 52.

MANDARIN ORANGE BISCUITS

BISCUIT DOUGH
220 g butter *or* margarine, softened
65 g (125 ml) icing sugar, sifted
finely grated rind of one orange
12,5 ml cornflour
125 g (250 ml) flour, sifted
75 g (125 ml) self-raising flour, sifted

MANDARIN ORANGE FILLING
60 g butter *or* margarine, softened
100 g (200 ml) icing sugar, sifted
6 canned mandarin orange segments, puréed

TO COMPLETE
sifted icing sugar

Biscuit dough
Cream together butter, icing sugar and orange rind until light and fluffy. Add sifted flours, beat until smooth.

Place mixture in piping bag fitted with a large, star nozzle. Pipe 25 mm rosettes on to lightly greased baking trays.

Bake at 180°C, 10 to 12 minutes until pale golden brown. (Biscuits will spread slightly.) Cool on wire cooling racks.

Mandarin orange filling
Place butter and icing sugar in mixing bowl, beat well. Gradually add purée, mix well.

Sandwich biscuits together with filling. Dust with sifted icing sugar before serving.

Makes about 20 single biscuits or 10 pairs.

LEMON AND GRANADILLA TWISTS

BISCUIT DOUGH
60 g butter *or* margarine, softened
190 g (340 ml) self-raising flour, sifted
20 ml milk
65 g (80 ml) sugar
2 ml vanilla essence
1 egg, lightly beaten

LEMON AND GRANADILLA ICING
100 g (190 ml) icing sugar, sifted
12,5 ml lemon juice
25 ml granadilla pulp
finely grated rind of half a lemon

Rub butter into flour, set aside. Place milk and sugar in a small saucepan, stir over low heat until sugar dissolves, add vanilla essence. Gradually add egg and milk mixture to flour mixture, mix well.

Knead dough until smooth. Roll small pieces of dough into narrow, 130 mm-long pieces. Using two pieces of dough, twist securely. Press ends together, forming a circle.

Place on lightly greased baking tray, bake at 180°C, 10 to 15 minutes, until pale golden brown. Leave to cool on wire cooling rack.

Lemon and granadilla icing
Combine icing sugar, lemon juice, granadilla pulp and lemon rind in a mixing bowl, beat until smooth.

Dip top of each biscuit into icing, leave to set.

Makes about 20.

NUTTY BISCUITS

ALMOND CRESCENTS

250 g butter *or* margarine, softened
250 g (300 ml) castor sugar
1 extra-large egg, lightly beaten
5 ml almond essence
37,5 ml soured cream
500 g (4 x 250 ml) flour, sifted
1 beaten egg to glaze
50 g (100 ml) nibbed almonds
15 g (25 ml) icing sugar, sifted

Cream together butter and castor sugar until light and creamy. Add egg, almond essence and cream. Sift in flour, work into mixture to form a firm but pliable dough. Turn out on to a lightly floured surface, knead lightly. Break off small pieces of dough, form into crescent shapes. Place on greased and lined baking trays. Chill in refrigerator one hour. Brush with egg glaze, coat half the biscuits with nibbed almonds.

Bake all biscuits at 190°C, about 20 minutes, until firm and pale golden brown in colour. Cool slightly on trays, then remove to wire cooling racks to cool completely. Sift icing sugar over plain biscuits. Store in airtight container.

Makes about 55.

PRALINE DELIGHTS

CUSTARD
40 g (50 ml) sugar
25 g (50 ml) flour
2 egg-yolks
250 ml milk

BISCUIT DOUGH
125 g (250 ml) flour, sifted
100 g (200 ml) ground almonds
90 g butter *or* margarine, chilled and roughly chopped
5 ml vanilla essence
1 egg-yolk

PRALINE
80 g (100 ml) sugar
50 g (125 ml) slivered almonds

FILLING
125 g butter *or* margarine, softened
40 g (75 ml) icing sugar, sifted
10 ml vanilla essence
sifted icing sugar to sprinkle

1 **Custard** Combine sugar and flour in small saucepan. Beat together egg-yolks and milk, stir in gradually. When smooth, cook over medium heat, stirring continuously until mixture thickens. Reduce heat, simmer, stirring continuously, one minute. Remove from heat, cover with sheet of wetted greaseproof paper, set aside.

2 **Biscuit dough** Combine flour and almonds in food processor bowl. Add butter, process until well mixed. Add vanilla essence and egg-yolk. Process until firm dough is formed. Set aside.

3 **Praline** Place sugar in small frying-pan, shake until spread evenly over base of pan. Place over medium heat until sugar melts and turns golden brown. Place almonds in well-greased baking pan. Pour melted sugar evenly over almonds, leave to cool.

4 Roll out dough to 3 mm thickness on floured surface. Cut out 60 mm-diameter rounds, place 10 mm apart on lightly greased baking tray. Bake at 160°C, eight to 10 minutes, or until golden brown. Leave to cool on trays.

5 Transfer biscuits to wire cooling rack.

Filling Cream together butter and icing sugar. Add vanilla essence, beat until light and creamy. Continue to beat, add in spoonfuls of cooled custard, until smooth and creamy.

6 Crush praline in food processor or with rolling-pin. Spread out on plate. Sandwich two biscuits together with filling, spread a little more filling around sides, roll in praline.

To complete
Sift icing sugar over each biscuit, serve at once.

Makes 15 complete biscuits.

ALMOND AND PECAN PUFFS

250 g butter *or* margarine, softened
60 g (75 ml) sugar
250 g (500 ml) flour, sifted
60 g (125 ml) cornflour
salt
10 ml vanilla essence
100 g (250 ml) pecan nuts, chopped
125 g (250 ml) flaked almonds, crushed
icing sugar, sifted

Cream together butter and sugar, add sifted dry ingredients. Mix to shortbread consistency. Stir in vanilla essence.

Divide dough in two. Add pecan nuts to one half, almonds to the other. Roll each portion into walnut-sized balls, place on baking trays.

Bake at 150°C, 30 minutes. While still hot, roll in icing sugar, allow to cool on wire cooling rack.

Makes 60.

MACAROONS

250 g (300 ml) castor sugar
200 g (400 ml) ground almonds
2 egg-whites, lightly frothed
1 ml almond essence
100 g (250 ml) whole blanched almonds

Combine castor sugar and almonds in bowl. Stir in egg-whites and almond essence. Knead lightly. Form into balls, place on greased and lined baking trays, flatten slightly with a fork. (Add 20 g more ground almonds if mixture is too soft.)

Press whole almond into centre of each biscuit. Bake at 180°C, 12 to 15 minutes. Leave on trays a few minutes before removing to wire cooling racks to cool completely.

Makes about 26.

ALMOND WHIRLS

180 g butter *or* margarine, softened
75 g (90 ml) castor sugar
60 g almond paste (marzipan)
2 egg-yolks
10 ml brandy
225 g (450 ml) flour, sifted
sifted icing sugar for sprinkling
youngberry jam or apricot jam

Cream together butter and castor sugar until pale and fluffy. Mix together almond paste and egg-yolks with a fork, add brandy, mix well. Gradually add to butter mixture, beating continuously. Add sifted flour, mix well.

Place mixture in piping bag fitted with an open rose nozzle. Pipe 30 mm-diameter rounds on to a greased baking tray. Indent centre slightly, using back of a teaspoon.

Bake at 180 °C, 12 minutes. Cool on wire cooling rack. When cold, sprinkle with sifted icing sugar, then spoon a little jam into centre of each biscuit.

Makes 25.

PRALINE CREAMS

BISCUITS
180 g butter *or* margarine, softened
250 g (312,5 ml) sugar
1 egg, well beaten
7 ml vanilla essence
300 g (600 ml) flour, sifted
3 ml baking-powder
1 ml salt

Praline creams *(left)*; Almond whirls *(right)*

PRALINE FILLING
100 g (250 ml) blanched almonds
80 g (100 ml) sugar
100 g butter *or* margarine, softened

Biscuits
Cream butter, add sugar, beat until fluffy. Add egg and vanilla essence, blend well. Sift together dry ingredients, stir into mixture, mix well. Refrigerate one hour.

Roll out dough thinly on floured surface. Cut into 50 mm-diameter rounds with fluted cutter. Place on greased baking tray, bake at 180 °C, eight to 10 minutes.

Praline filling
In heavy saucepan, cook almonds and sugar over low heat until sugar caramelises, stirring occasionally. Immediately pour on to greased baking tray.

When cool and hard, crush into a powder in plastic bag with rolling-pin. Cream butter until fluffy, beat in praline a little at a time until smooth and thick.

Sandwich biscuits together with praline filling. Filling can be coloured pink or green if desired.

Makes 46 single biscuits or 23 pairs.

HONEY ALMOND BISCUITS

Honey almond biscuits *(right)*; Almond fruit slice *(left)*; Nutty chocolate squares *(bottom)*

FILLING
130 g (80 ml) liquid honey
65 g (80 ml) sugar
90 ml brandy
100 g (250 ml) blanched almonds, finely chopped
100 g (250 ml) walnuts, finely chopped
60 g (120 ml) ground almonds
40 g (60 ml) raisins
15 ml finely grated orange rind
1 ml ground cloves
1 ml ground nutmeg
3 ml ground cinnamon
1 ml almond essence

DOUGH
310 g (625 ml) flour, sifted
80 g (100 ml) sugar
7 ml oil
75 g butter *or* margarine, softened
75 ml milk
75 ml brandy
1 egg, beaten
halved blanched almonds to decorate

54

Filling
Heat honey over low heat in heavy saucepan, add sugar, brandy, almonds, walnuts and ground almonds. Add raisins, orange rind and spices, mix well. Remove saucepan from heat, set aside.

Dough
Sift flour into a bowl, mix in sugar, work in oil and butter, moisten with milk and brandy to form a firm but pliable dough.

Roll out dough on floured surface into a rectangle of 3 mm thickness. Trim edges. Cut dough into three strips, each 100 mm wide. Brush surface of strips with beaten egg.

Divide filling into three portions, spoon down centre of each strip. Roll up dough tightly around filling, trim edges. Place rolls on greased baking trays, seam-side down. Glaze with beaten egg, press almonds diagonally into top of each roll.

Bake at 180 °C, 25 to 30 minutes. Remove from oven, loosen with spatula and leave to cool on baking tray. Slice diagonally into biscuits.

Makes about 60.

ALMOND FRUIT SLICE

PASTRY
225 g (450 ml) flour, sifted
pinch of salt
100 g butter *or* margarine
50 ml cold water

FILLING
150 g butter *or* margarine, softened
150 g (180 ml) castor sugar
2 eggs, beaten
1 ml almond essence
100 g (200 ml) ground almonds
115 g (230 ml) flour, sifted
75 g (115 ml) glacé cherries, chopped
25 g (40 ml) blanched almonds, roughly chopped
75 g (125 ml) sultanas
25 g (60 ml) flaked almonds
castor sugar for sprinkling

Sift together flour and salt, rub in butter until mixture resembles breadcrumbs. Add water, mix together with round-bladed knife to form a firm dough.

Using fingertips, gently knead dough on a lightly floured surface until smooth and free of cracks. Roll out pastry into a rectangle large enough to line base and sides of a 350 mm by 210 mm swiss roll pan, trim edges.

Filling
Cream together butter and castor sugar until pale and fluffy, add eggs with a little of the flour to prevent curdling. Add almond essence and beat well. Stir in ground almonds, flour, cherries, chopped almonds and sultanas, mix well. Spoon filling into pastry-lined pan, spread evenly.

Sprinkle surface with flaked almonds, bake at 180 °C, 35 to 40 minutes, until firm. Cool in pan, sprinkle with castor sugar. Cut into bars.

Makes 30 to 35 bars.

NUTTY CHOCOLATE SQUARES

175 g (350 ml) flour, sifted
10 g (25 ml) cocoa powder
50 g (100 ml) custard powder
175 g butter *or* margarine, softened
75 g (90 ml) castor sugar

TOPPING
75 g butter *or* margarine
75 g (105 ml) soft brown sugar
20 g (12,5 ml) liquid honey
2 ml almond essence
100 g (250 ml) unsalted nuts, chopped and toasted
100 g dark chocolate, melted

Sift flour, cocoa powder and custard powder into a large mixing bowl. Rub in butter with fingertips until mixture becomes sticky. Add castor sugar, continue rubbing with fingertips until mixture can be pressed into a ball. (Alternatively, prepare dough in food processor.) Knead lightly until smooth.

Press dough into a greased and base-lined 180 mm-square cake pan. Prick with a fork.

Bake at 160 °C, 60 to 75 minutes, or until golden brown. Cool in pan 10 minutes. Carefully turn out on to wire cooling rack, peel off paper and leave to cool completely.

Topping
Melt butter, brown sugar and honey in a saucepan over low heat. Boil three minutes, stirring continuously. Remove from heat. Add almond essence and nuts, mix well. Spread mixture over biscuit base, leave to set 20 minutes.

Cut into squares, leave until firm, a further 30 minutes. Brush melted chocolate over top of each square. Allow to set before serving.

Makes 16.

CHOCOLATE AND COFFEE BISCUITS

Chocolate and vanilla spirals *(left)*; Chocolate and orange cookies *(centre)*; Choc-chip cookies *(right)*

CHOCOLATE ORANGE COOKIES

100 g plain chocolate
125 g butter *or* margarine, softened
125 g (150 ml) castor sugar
pinch of salt
1 egg, beaten
grated rind of one orange
200 g (400 ml) flour, sifted
5 ml baking-powder

ICING
100 g (200 ml) icing sugar, sifted
25 ml orange juice
finely shredded orange rind to decorate

Coarsely grate chocolate. Cream together butter and castor sugar, add salt, egg and orange rind. Sift flour and baking-powder into creamed mixture, add chocolate. Knead all ingredients together into a dough. Wrap in foil and chill two hours in refrigerator.

Roll out dough to 5 mm thickness and cut out rounds 50 mm in diameter. Place on greased baking trays, allowing room for spreading, and bake at 200°C, 10 to 15 minutes. Carefully remove from baking trays, leave to cool on a wire cooling rack.

Icing
Sift icing sugar into a bowl. Add orange juice gradually, beat until smooth. Spread over top of cookies and leave to set. Decorate with shredded orange rind if desired.

Makes 30.

CHOCOLATE AND VANILLA SPIRALS

250 g butter *or* margarine, softened
200 g (250 ml) sugar
2 eggs, beaten
25 ml rum essence
480 g (960 ml) flour, sifted
3 ml baking-powder
15 g (37,5 ml) cocoa powder, sifted
1 egg-white, lightly beaten

Cream together butter and sugar until light and fluffy. Add eggs and rum essence, beat well. Sift in flour and baking-powder, mix well to form a firm dough.

Divide dough in half, knead cocoa powder into one half, mix well. Wrap each portion in clingwrap, refrigerate one hour or until firm.

Roll out each piece of dough separately to 6 mm thickness. Brush one piece with egg-white, place other piece on top. Brush again with egg-white. Starting at one long side, roll up as for swiss roll. Wrap tightly in wax-paper, refrigerate until firm.

Cut into 6 mm slices, place on greased baking trays. Bake at 180°C, 12 to 15 minutes or until firm to the touch. Remove to wire cooling rack to cool.

Makes 50.

CHOC-CHIP COOKIES

300 g butter *or* margarine, softened
375 g (445 ml) castor sugar
600 g (1 200 ml) flour, sifted
140 ml milk
5 ml vanilla essence
70 g (45 ml) golden syrup
150 g chocolate morsels

Place first six ingredients in a mixing bowl. Mix with electric beater until dough forms a soft ball. Stir in chocolate morsels, knead five minutes.

Roll dough into small balls, place on greased baking trays, flatten with a fork. Refrigerate 30 minutes.

Bake at 180°C, 12 to 15 minutes or until golden brown. Remove to wire cooling rack to cool.

Makes about 90 biscuits.

CHOC-WHEAT BISCUITS

240 g (480 ml) wholewheat flour, sifted and husks replaced
5 ml baking-powder
2 ml salt
120 g butter *or* margarine, softened
60 g (75 ml) castor sugar
1 egg, lightly beaten
120 g dark chocolate, melted
120 g white chocolate, melted

Combine flour, baking-powder and salt in a mixing bowl. Rub in butter. Stir in castor sugar. Add egg, mix well to form a firm dough.

Roll out dough on a lightly floured surface. Cut out rounds using a 50 mm-diameter cutter. Place on greased baking trays.

Bake at 220 °C, 10 minutes or until pale golden brown. Leave to cool on a wire cooling rack.

Spread melted dark chocolate over one side of each biscuit. Spoon melted white chocolate into greaseproof paper piping bag, pipe regularly spaced stripes across biscuits. Pull knife point or skewer through chocolate while still wet. Work in opposite direction each time to create a 'feathered' effect. Allow to set.

Makes 40 to 45 biscuits.

SILKY CHOCOLATE SQUARES

BASE
140 g (280 ml) flour, sifted
15 g (37,5 ml) cocoa powder, sifted
100 g butter *or* margarine, softened
50 g (125 ml) pecan nuts, chopped
30 g (37,5 ml) brown sugar

FILLING
125 g butter *or* margarine, softened
150 g (180 ml) castor sugar
2 eggs, beaten
100 g milk chocolate, melted
75 g (125 ml) seedless raisins, finely chopped

TO COMPLETE
5 ml instant coffee powder
250 ml fresh cream
20 g (25 ml) castor sugar
50 g milk chocolate, melted

Base
Combine all ingredients in food processor until a soft dough is formed. Press mixture into greased and lined 170 mm by 280 mm lamington pan. Bake at 180 °C, 15 minutes or until cooked and firm to the touch. Leave in pan to cool completely.

Filling
Cream together butter and castor sugar until light and fluffy. Gradually add eggs, beat well. Stir in chocolate and raisins until combined. Spread chocolate mixture over cooled base, refrigerate three hours or until firm.

To complete
Mix coffee powder with 12,5 ml cream, add to remaining cream together with castor sugar, beat until stiff. Spread cream over filling, freeze until firm. When firm, cut into squares and decorate each square by drizzling with melted chocolate. Serve straight from freezer.

Makes 24 bars.

CRISP AND CREAMY CHOCOLATE SURPRISES

2 extra-large eggs, separated
1 egg-white
50 g (100 ml) flour, sifted
75 g (150 ml) cornflour
pinch of salt
60 g (75 ml) castor sugar

FILLING
250 ml milk
15 g (25 ml) custard powder
30 g (37,5 ml) castor sugar
12,5 ml Grand Marnier liqueur (optional)
125 ml cream, whipped

TOPPING
125 g dark chocolate
2 ml oil

TO COMPLETE
• thick white glacé icing (optional)

To complete
Pipe zigzag lines of white glacé or royal icing over tops of biscuits if desired. Leave to set before serving.

Makes 12 single biscuits or six pairs.

1 Combine egg-yolks, one egg-white, flour, cornflour and salt in large mixing bowl. Beat well five minutes, until mixture is stiff. Whisk together remaining egg-whites and castor sugar until soft peaks form. Fold into egg-yolk mixture.

2 Spoon mixture into a piping bag fitted with a 10 mm plain nozzle. Grease and line a baking tray with greaseproof paper and outline 40 mm circles on paper. Pipe mixture inside circles, building up centres slightly. Bake at 200 °C, 15 minutes.

Filling
Combine milk, custard powder and castor sugar in a small saucepan. Bring to the boil, cook a few minutes. Add liqueur. Cool. Fold in cream, chill.

3 Remove biscuits from baking tray. Using a teaspoon, hollow out inside of each biscuit.

4 Gently grate top side of six biscuits making them slightly flatter, enabling them to stand.

5 Spoon chilled filling into a piping bag fitted with a small rose nozzle. Pipe a little filling into each hollow biscuit. Sandwich two biscuits together.

6 Place on wire cooling rack, flat-side down. Melt chocolate with oil in bowl over hot water. Coat each biscuit with chocolate. Leave to set.

COFFEE AND PECAN-NUT BISCUITS

220 g (440 ml) flour, sifted
125 g butter *or* margarine, cut up
50 g (60 ml) sugar
1 egg, lightly beaten
5 ml vanilla essence

PECAN-NUT FILLING
60 g butter *or* margarine, softened
30 g (60 ml) icing sugar, sifted
80 g (200 ml) pecan-nuts, finely chopped
12,5 ml milk

COFFEE ICING
190 g (375 ml) icing sugar, sifted
5 ml butter, softened
12,5 ml instant coffee powder, dissolved in
12,5 ml boiling water
20 ml milk

TO DECORATE
12 pecan-nut halves

Sift flour into a mixing bowl, rub in butter until mixture resembles fine breadcrumbs. Add sugar, egg and vanilla essence, mix to form a soft dough. Roll out on a lightly floured surface to 5 mm thickness. Cut out rounds using a 60 mm-diameter plain biscuit cutter. Place on a lightly greased baking tray, bake at 180 °C, about 20 minutes, until pale golden brown. Cool on wire cooling racks.

Pecan-nut filling
Cream butter until light and fluffy, add icing sugar, beat well. Add pecan-nuts and milk, stir well. Spread half the biscuits with filling, top with remaining biscuits, refrigerate 30 minutes.

Coffee icing
Place icing sugar in top of double-boiler, add butter, dissolved coffee and milk. Beat over simmering water until smooth. Remove from heat, leave to cool slightly. Beat well. Spread over top of each biscuit. Place half a pecan-nut in centre of each biscuit. Leave to set.

Makes about 11 pairs.

COFFEE KISSES

200 g (360 ml) self-raising flour, sifted
90 g (112,5 ml) sugar
90 g butter *or* margarine, softened
1 egg, beaten
20 ml coffee essence *or* coffee liqueur *(see note)*

FILLING
half quantity Coffee cream filling *(see recipe)*

Sift flour into processor bowl. Add sugar and butter, blend until fine breadcrumbs form. Add egg and coffee essence, blend until a firm dough forms and leaves sides of bowl clean.

Turn out on to a lightly floured surface, knead gently. Wrap in wax-paper, refrigerate two hours or overnight.

Form dough into walnut-sized balls. Place on lightly greased baking trays, bake at 180 °C, 15 to 20 minutes. Remove to wire cooling rack to cool completely.

Sandwich together with **Coffee cream filling**.

Makes 36 single biscuits or 18 pairs.

COFFEE FINGER BISCUITS

12,5 ml instant coffee powder
50 ml boiling water
250 g butter *or* margarine, softened
50 g (60 ml) castor sugar
250 g (500 ml) flour, sifted
pinch of salt

FILLING AND DECORATION
one quantity Coffee cream filling *(see recipe)*
125 g dark cooking chocolate

Dissolve coffee powder in boiling water. Cream together butter and castor sugar until light and fluffy. Add dissolved coffee, fold in flour and salt. Fill large piping bag fitted with star nozzle and pipe 75 mm-lengths of mixture on to greased and lined baking trays. Bake at 200 °C, 12 to 15 minutes. Remove and cool on wire cooling racks. Sandwich biscuits together with filling. Melt chocolate in top of double-boiler over gently simmering water without stirring. Remove from heat. Dip one end of each biscuit pair into chocolate and leave to dry on sheet of wax-paper.

Makes about 30 single biscuits or 15 pairs.

COFFEE CREAM BISCUITS

125 g butter *or* margarine, softened
50 g (60 ml) sugar
5 ml instant coffee powder
1 egg, beaten
5 ml vanilla essence
190 g (375 ml) flour, sifted

FILLING AND DECORATION
two-thirds quantity Coffee cream filling *(see recipe)*
sifted icing sugar

Cream together butter and sugar until pale and fluffy. Beat in coffee powder. Add beaten egg and vanilla essence. Mix in sifted flour to form a stiff dough. (May also be prepared in food processor if preferred.) Turn out dough on to lightly floured surface, knead gently until smooth. Roll out thinly, cut into shapes, place on lightly greased baking trays. Bake at 180 °C, 10 to 12 minutes. Remove to wire cooling racks to cool completely. Sandwich together with Coffee cream filling. Sift icing sugar over tops just before serving.

Makes 40 single biscuits or 20 pairs.

COFFEE CREAM FILLING

90 g butter *or* margarine, softened
130 g (250 ml) icing sugar, sifted
5 ml instant coffee powder
15 ml coffee essence *or* coffee liqueur
little milk *or* cream if necessary

Beat butter in a bowl until creamy, add icing sugar and instant coffee. Cream together. Beat in essence using a wooden spoon. Add more sifted icing sugar, if necessary, to produce a smooth, spreadable consistency. Add milk if icing is too firm. Cover and store in refrigerator until needed. Leave standing at room temperature and beat well before using.

Note If you don't have coffee essence or coffee liqueur, dissolve 10 ml instant coffee powder in 10 ml boiling water, add 3 ml castor sugar, stir well. Allow to cool. Use as a substitute for essence or liqueur in the recipes.

In front of biscuit jar: Coffee kisses. In basket: Coffee finger biscuits *(left)*; and Coffee cream biscuits *(right)*

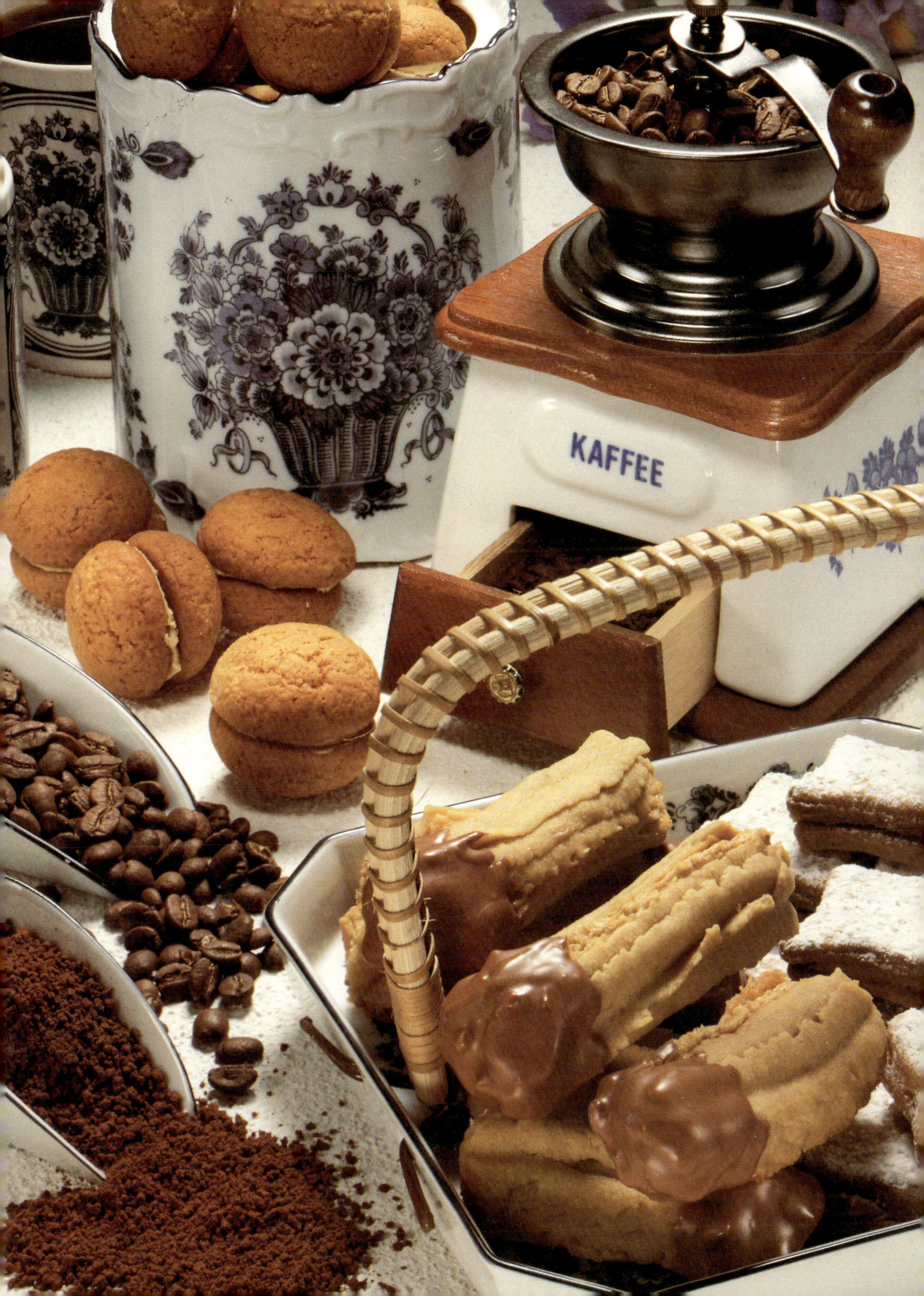
KAFFEE

COFFEE HAZEL-NUT BISCUITS

COFFEE BUTTER CREAM
125 g butter *or* margarine, softened
5 ml vanilla essence
130 g (250 ml) icing sugar, sifted
10 ml instant coffee powder
10 ml hot water
10 ml milk

BISCUITS
190 g butter *or* margarine
50 g (60 ml) sugar
5 ml instant coffee powder
5 ml boiling water
60 g (200 ml) roasted hazel-nuts, finely chopped
250 g (500 ml) flour, sifted

TO COMPLETE
90 g dark chocolate
30 g white margarine

1 Coffee butter cream Beat butter and vanilla essence until light and creamy. Gradually add icing sugar, beat until well combined. Dissolve coffee in hot water, cool, add to creamed mixture with milk, mix well. Set aside.

2 Biscuits Cream together butter and sugar until light and fluffy. Dissolve coffee in boiling water, cool. Add to creamed mixture, mix well. Add hazel-nuts and flour, mix well, refrigerate 30 minutes.

Roll out dough thinly on a floured surface, cut into circles with 35 mm- and 50 mm-diameter cutters. Cut equal amounts of each size.

3 Place on greased baking trays, bake at 180°C, 10 to 15 minutes or until light golden in colour. Remove from trays, cool on wire cooling rack. Pipe rosettes of Coffee butter cream over surface of large biscuits.

4 Melt chocolate and white margarine in top of double-boiler over gently simmering water, allow to cool slightly. Pour into saucer, dip one side of each small biscuit into chocolate mixture, leave on wax-paper to dry. Place a small chocolate-coated biscuit on top of each large biscuit.

Serve within one hour of completion.

Makes about 15 complete biscuits.

SAVOURY BISCUITS

SAVOURY CHEESE BISCUITS

90 g butter *or* margarine, softened
125 g (250 ml) flour, sifted
pinch of cayenne pepper
2 ml dry mustard powder
2 extra-large egg-yolks
100 g (250 ml) Cheddar cheese, grated
1 extra-large egg-white, lightly frothed
poppy seeds, sesame seeds and caraway seeds

Beat butter until soft and creamy. Sift together flour, cayenne and mustard, add to butter. Mix in egg-yolks and cheese. Mix to form a stiff dough, knead lightly. Turn out on to a lightly floured surface and roll out to 5 mm thickness. Using 50 mm-diameter cutters, cut into various shapes. Brush biscuits with egg-white, sprinkle with seeds. Place on lightly greased baking trays, bake at 180 °C, about 20 minutes until pale golden brown. Cool and store in an airtight tin.

Makes about 40 biscuits.

DANISH BLUE BITES

60 g butter *or* margarine, softened
90 g (180 ml) flour, sifted
60 g (125 ml) blue-veined cheese, grated
salt and pepper
5 ml dry mustard powder
1 egg, beaten
60 g (150 ml) walnuts, chopped
paprika

Rub butter into flour until mixture resembles fine breadcrumbs. Add cheese and seasoning to taste. Mix in mustard. Stir in enough egg to give a firm dough. Knead until smooth. Roll out on a floured surface, cut into assorted shapes. Place on a greased baking tray. Brush with remaining egg. Sprinkle with nuts and paprika. Bake at 180 °C, 10 to 12 minutes. Allow to cool on wire cooling rack.

Makes about 20.

CRISPY CHEESE BISCUITS

120 g butter, creamed
100 g (250 ml) Cheddar cheese, grated
2 ml salt
2 ml cayenne pepper
140 g (250 ml) self-raising flour, sifted
80 g (250 ml) crushed cornflakes
1 egg, beaten
25 ml milk
10 g (25 ml) grated Parmesan cheese

Combine butter, Cheddar cheese, salt and cayenne pepper. Mix well. Add flour and cornflakes. Whisk together egg and milk. Add to flour mixture to form a soft dough.

Roll mixture into walnut-sized balls. Place on lightly greased baking trays. Press down lightly with a fork. Sprinkle with Parmesan cheese.

Bake at 180 °C, 10 to 15 minutes. Allow to cool on a wire cooling rack.

Makes about 36.

JUGGLER'S CHEESE STICKS

250 g (500 ml) flour, sifted
pinch of salt
125 g butter *or* margarine, softened
125 g (310 ml) Cheddar cheese, grated
1 egg-yolk
iced water
paprika

Sift flour and salt into a mixing bowl. Rub in butter until mixture resembles fine breadcrumbs. Stir in cheese. Make well in centre, stir in egg-yolk and enough iced water to make a stiff dough.
Wrap in wax-paper, refrigerate 30 minutes. Turn out on to a lightly floured surface. Roll out pastry between two sheets of greaseproof paper to about 5 mm thickness (or use the Doughmaster plastic sheets).

Using ruler as a guide, cut sticks 10 mm wide and 150 mm long. Twist each stick gently to form a spiral. Place on lightly greased baking trays and sprinkle with paprika.

Bake at 200 °C, 10 to 12 minutes, until pale golden brown. Remove from baking trays and place on wire cooling racks to cool completely. Store in airtight tin. Crisp up in low oven when required.

Makes about 24.

TANGY MUSTARD NIBBLES

100 g (200 ml) flour, sifted
5 ml salt
2 ml paprika
pinch of cayenne pepper
60 g butter *or* margarine, cut up
10 ml dry mustard powder
100 g (250 ml) Cheddar cheese, finely grated
1 egg, lightly beaten

Sift together flour, salt, paprika and cayenne pepper into food processor bowl. Add butter and process a few minutes until mixture resembles fine breadcrumbs. Add mustard and cheese. Add egg and process a further few seconds until mixture forms a stiff dough.

Turn out on to a lightly floured surface, roll out to 4 mm thickness. Cut into 30 mm squares.

Place on lightly greased baking trays, bake at 200 °C, 10 minutes or until pale golden brown. Cool on wire cooling rack.

Makes about 36.

Tangy mustard nibbles (left); Juggler's cheese sticks (right)

MIXED BAG

APPLE AND ALMOND SQUARES

125 g butter *or* margarine, softened
65 g (125 ml) icing sugar, sifted
125 g (250 ml) flour, sifted
60 g (125 ml) custard powder
15 g (25 ml) dried milk powder
12,5 ml water

FILLING
 2 Granny Smith apples, peeled, cored and thinly sliced
165 g (125 ml) plum jam, warmed
1 egg
50 g (60 ml) castor sugar
35 g (60 ml) self-raising flour, sifted
40 g (125 ml) desiccated coconut
12,5 ml lemon juice
37,5 ml cream
60 g (150 ml) flaked almonds

Cream together butter and icing sugar. Sift together remaining dry ingredients, add to mixture. Add water and knead dough on a lightly floured surface. Wrap in clingwrap, refrigerate 30 minutes. Roll out dough to 3 mm thickness.

Cover base of greased 280 mm by 180 mm lamington pan.

Filling
Arrange apple slices on dough, spread with jam. Beat egg lightly, gradually add castor sugar, beating well after each addition. Add flour, coconut, lemon juice and cream, mix well. Pour this mixture over apples and jam, spread evenly to cover surface. Sprinkle with almonds.

Bake at 180 °C, 35 to 40 minutes, or until golden brown and firm. Cut into squares while warm.

Makes 18 squares.

COCONUT MELTING MOMENTS

220 g (440 ml) flour, sifted
40 g (80 ml) cornflour, sifted
105 g (125 ml) castor sugar
250 g butter *or* margarine, softened
80 g (250 ml) desiccated coconut
18 glacé cherries, halved

Place flour, cornflour and castor sugar in food processor, blend in butter until a soft dough is formed. Refrigerate one hour until firm. Form into small balls, roll in coconut, place on lightly greased baking trays. Place half a cherry in centre of each round, push down slightly.

Bake at 150 °C, 20 to 25 minutes or until lightly browned.

Makes about 30 to 35.

MARSHMALLOW BISCUITS

60 g butter *or* margarine, softened
100 g (125 ml) sugar
1 egg-yolk
3 ml vanilla essence
10 ml milk
105 g (190 ml) self-raising flour, sifted
30 g (60 ml) flour, sifted
80 g (60 ml) raspberry jam
750 g (about 9 x 250 ml) desiccated coconut

MARSHMALLOW
200 g (250 ml) sugar
250 ml water
15 g (20 ml) gelatine
3 ml vanilla essence
red food colouring

CHOCOLATE COATING
180 g dark cooking chocolate
30 g white margarine

1 Cream together butter and sugar very well until light and fluffy. Add egg-yolk, vanilla essence and milk, beat well. Sift in flours to form a stiff dough. Turn out on to a lightly floured surface, knead until smooth ball forms. Wrap and refrigerate 30 minutes. Roll out dough to 3 mm thickness and cut into 40 mm-diameter rounds, using a plain cutter.

2 Place on greased baking trays and bake at 180°C, eight to 10 minutes, until golden brown. Cool on wire cooling racks. Spread base of each biscuit with about 3 ml jam.

3 Pour coconut into large deep dish, about 50 mm deep. Spread out coconut evenly. Press a large egg halfway down into coconut to make about 12 hollows, 25 mm apart.

4 **Marshmallow** Place sugar and water in a saucepan, sprinkle gelatine over surface, heat gently, stirring, until sugar has dissolved. Bring to the boil, reduce heat, simmer seven minutes. Remove from heat, allow to cool. Pour into bowl of electric mixer, add vanilla essence, beat three minutes until thick and fluffy. Add a few drops of red food colouring to colour marshmallow pink.

5 Carefully spoon about 12,5 ml marshmallow into each coconut hollow, filling hollows to the top.

6 Place a biscuit, jam-side down, on top of marshmallow and press down firmly. Leave two minutes, lift biscuits gently: marshmallow will adhere to each biscuit. Fill hollows with remaining marshmallow and repeat process with remaining biscuits.

7 To coat biscuits with chocolate, melt chocolate with margarine in the top of a double-boiler without stirring. Allow chocolate to cool completely but still remain liquid before dipping biscuits, or marshmallow will melt. Dip biscuits, marshmallow-side down, into chocolate and coat completely. Place on greaseproof paper to dry and harden.

Makes about 30 biscuits.

MEALIE-MEAL BISCUITS

190 g (375 ml) flour, sifted
5 ml baking-powder
60 g (125 ml) mealie-meal
1 ml salt
80 g butter *or* margarine, softened
40 g (125 ml) desiccated coconut
150 g (190 ml) sugar
1 large egg, beaten
25 ml - 50 ml milk
12 glacé cherries, quartered

Sift together flour, baking-powder, mealie-meal and salt. Rub in butter with fingertips. Stir in coconut and sugar. Beat egg with 25 ml milk, stir into dry ingredients, adding a little more milk if necessary to form a firm dough.
Roll out thinly on a lightly floured surface, cut into fancy shapes using biscuit cutters. Press a quarter cherry into the centre of each. Chill 20 minutes before baking at 190°C, 10 to 12 minutes. Remove to wire cooling racks to cool completely. Store in an airtight tin.
Makes about 45.

ALMOND COCONUT SLICES

PASTRY BASE
170 g (340 ml) flour, sifted
20 g (25 ml) castor sugar
5 ml baking-powder
60 g butter *or* margarine, softened
1 egg-yolk
25 ml cold water

FILLING	**GLACÉ ICING**
60 g butter *or* margarine, softened	130 g (250 ml) icing sugar, sifted
50 g (60 ml) castor sugar	boiling water to mix
1 egg, beaten	
3 ml almond essence	
60 g (200 ml) desiccated coconut	

Pastry base
Sift dry ingredients into a mixing bowl, rub in butter. Mix egg-yolk with water, add to dry ingredients. Using a round-bladed knife, cut into mixture to form a smooth dough. Roll out on a lightly floured surface to 4 mm thickness. Trim into a rectangle to fit base of a lightly greased 300 mm by 240 mm baking try. Reserve excess pastry for lattice.

Filling
Cream together butter and castor sugar in a bowl, add egg, continue to beat until mixture is fluffy. Add almond essence, fold in coconut. Spread mixture over pastry base, cover with strips of pastry to form a lattice. Bake at 190°C, 25 to 30 minutes or until risen and lightly browned. Remove from oven, leave to cool.

Glacé icing
Combine icing sugar and boiling water in a small bowl to form a smooth icing, spread over lattice evenly. Cut into slices.

Makes 24 slices.

CEREAL

CRUNCHY CHOCOLATE BISCUITS

440 g butter *or* margarine, softened
240 g (300 ml) sugar
400 g (800 ml) flour, sifted
10 g (25 ml) cocoa powder, sifted
200 g (550 ml) rolled oats
200 g (625 ml) desiccated coconut
5 ml baking-powder

CHOCOLATE ICING
250 g (480 ml) icing sugar, sifted
10 g (25 ml) cocoa powder, sifted
about 60 ml warm water

Cream together butter and sugar until light and fluffy. Add remaining ingredients to form a soft dough. Roll dough into small balls with floured hands.

Place on greased baking trays, flatten slightly with a fork. Bake at 180°C, 15 to 20 minutes.

Chocolate icing
Sift icing sugar and cocoa powder into a bowl, gradually add warm water to obtain a smooth, runny consistency.

Remove biscuits from oven, place on wire cooling rack. Drizzle with chocolate icing while still warm. Allow to dry and cool completely, store in airtight container.

Makes 80.

CRISPY CHOCOLATE FINGERS

300 g (600 ml) flour, sifted
100 g (120 ml) castor sugar
200 g butter *or* margarine, softened

TOPPING
160 g milk chocolate, melted
40 g (250 ml) Rice Krispies

Sift flour into a mixing bowl. Stir in castor sugar. Rub in butter with fingertips until mixture sticks together. Knead gently. Press dough into lightly greased 175 mm by 270 mm swiss roll pan.

Bake at 180°C, 20 to 25 minutes. Leave to cool in pan.

Topping
Pour melted chocolate into a bowl, stir in Rice Krispies.

Spread topping over biscuit base. Leave to set. Cut into fingers to serve.

Makes 18 fingers.

PECAN CORNFLAKE COOKIES

125 g butter *or* margarine
90 g (125 ml) soft brown sugar
105 g (125 ml) castor sugar
60 g (125 ml) flour, sifted
40 g (125 ml) desiccated coconut
150 g (750 ml) lightly crushed cornflakes
1 extra-large egg, lightly beaten
50 g (125 ml) pecan nuts *or* walnuts, finely chopped
80 g (125 ml) glacé cherries, quartered

Melt butter, stir in brown sugar, castor sugar and flour. Remove from heat. Add coconut and cornflakes. Stir in beaten egg, nuts and cherries, mix well.

Place spoonfuls of mixture far apart on lightly greased baking trays. Press lightly together with fingertips.

Bake at 180 °C, 10 to 12 minutes until golden brown. Leave on trays to cool for a minute or two, then remove to wire cooling racks to cool completely. Serve within a few hours of baking.

Makes about 35.

CHEWY NUT BARS

100 ml oil
120 g (75 ml) liquid honey
100 g (137,5 ml) soft brown sugar
200 g (550 ml) rolled oats
50 g (160 ml) desiccated coconut
50 g (85 ml) sesame seeds
50 g (125 ml) flaked almonds, finely chopped
50 g (125 ml) hazel-nuts, finely chopped

Place oil and honey in a bowl, add brown sugar, mix well. Add remaining ingredients, stir well to combine. Press mixture into lightly greased 330 mm by 230 mm swiss roll pan.

Bake at 180 °C, 25 to 30 minutes, or until golden brown. Leave to cool in pan for five minutes before marking into bars. Allow to cool completely before removing from pan. Store in an airtight tin.

Makes 30 bars.

SEED BISCUITS

80 g (300 ml) rolled oats
40 g (65 ml) oat bran *or* 10g (65 ml) digestive bran
250 g (500 ml) flour, sifted
400 g (500 ml) sugar
pinch of salt
250 g butter *or* margarine
80 g (50 ml) golden syrup
50 ml water
7 ml bicarbonate of soda
60 g (100 ml) sesame seeds
15 g (25 ml) aniseed (optional)
30 g (45 ml) poppy seeds
80 g (150 ml) sunflower seeds

Combine oats, bran, flour, sugar and salt in a large mixing bowl, set aside. Melt butter, syrup and water in a small saucepan over low heat. Remove from heat, stir in bicarbonate of soda until mixture froths. Add to dry ingredients with seeds, stir well.

Using hands, form mixture into small balls, place on lightly greased baking trays, flatten with a fork. Bake at 180 °C, 15 to 20 minutes, or until evenly browned. Leave on trays to cool and harden. Remove to wire cooling racks to cool completely. Store in airtight tin.

Makes about 70 biscuits.

PINEAPPLE SANDWICH CRUNCHIES

360 g (4 x 250 ml) rolled oats
260 g butter *or* margarine, melted
50 g (100 ml) flour
50 ml milk
280 g (350 ml) sugar
5 ml salt
375 ml grated apple
265 g (200 ml) pineapple jam

Combine first seven ingredients in a mixing bowl. Pour half the mixture into a lightly greased 270 mm by 370 mm swiss roll pan, press down firmly.

Spread jam over base, cover with remaining oat mixture.

Bake at 190 °C, 30 to 40 minutes, until top is crisp and brown. Allow to cool in pan. Cut into squares for serving.

Makes 35 squares.

Seed biscuits *(left)*; Chewy nut bars *(centre)*; Pineapple sandwich crunchies *(right)*

AFGHANS

200 g butter *or* margarine, softened
90 g (105 ml) castor sugar
180 g (360 ml) flour, sifted
pinch of salt
10 g (25 ml) cocoa powder, sifted
60 g (300 ml) lightly crushed cornflakes

TO DECORATE
60 g chocolate, melted

Cream together butter and castor sugar until light and fluffy. Sift flour, salt and cocoa into a bowl, work into creamed mixture. Stir in cornflakes.

Place 12,5 ml mounds on to greased and lined baking trays. Bake at 180 °C, 12 to 15 minutes. Cool on wire cooling racks.

To decorate
Spoon melted chocolate into piping bag fitted with a No 2 writing nozzle, drizzle chocolate over biscuits. Allow to set. Store in airtight container.

Makes about 20.

SLICES

On plate: Banana pecan squares (left); Apple sauce bars (right)

BANANA PECAN SQUARES

125 g butter *or* margarine, softened
150 g (180 ml) castor sugar
1 egg, beaten
5 ml vanilla essence
250 ml mashed banana (3 to 4 small bananas)
190 g (375 ml) flour, sifted
2 ml bicarbonate of soda
2 ml salt
50 g (125 ml) pecan nuts, chopped
16 pecan halves

Cream together butter and castor sugar until pale and fluffy. Beat in egg, vanilla essence and bananas. Sift together flour, bicarbonate of soda and salt, fold into creamed mixture. Add chopped nuts, mix well. Spread mixture into a greased 220 mm-square pan, mark lightly into 16 squares, place pecan halves in centre of each square.

Bake at 180 °C, about 40 minutes, or until a skewer inserted into the centre comes out clean. Remove from oven, leave to cool in pan five minutes before turning out on to a wooden board. Cut into squares, leave to cool on wire cooling rack.

Makes 16 squares.

APPLE SAUCE BARS

2 cooking apples, peeled, cored and quartered
50 ml water
250 g (500 ml) flour, sifted
210 g (250 ml) castor sugar
2 ml salt
5 ml bicarbonate of soda
5 ml ground cinnamon
2 ml ground nutmeg
1 egg, beaten
125 g butter *or* margarine, softened
2 ml vanilla essence
150 g (250 ml) raisins
100 g (250 ml) walnuts, chopped (*optional*)

GLACÉ ICING
130 g (250 ml) icing sugar, sifted
10 ml instant coffee powder, dissolved in
15 ml - 20 ml boiling water

Place apples with water in small saucepan, cook over very low heat until tender, purée.

Sift dry ingredients into a large bowl. Beat in egg, butter and vanilla essence until well blended. Stir in raisins, nuts and apple purée.

Pour into a greased and lined 280 mm by 180 mm baking tray, spreading evenly. Bake at 180 °C, about 40 minutes, or until top springs back when pressed with fingertips. Turn out on to wire cooling rack and remove paper.

Glacé icing
Combine icing sugar and instant coffee to make a thick coating consistency. Spread over warm cake. Cut into bars when icing has set.

Makes about 24 bars.

COCONUT AND ALMOND SQUARES

BASE
200 g (355 ml) self-raising flour, sifted
80 g butter *or* margarine, softened
80 g (90 ml) castor sugar
1 egg, beaten
37,5 ml milk
130 g (100 ml) smooth apricot jam, warmed

TOPPING
100 g (180 ml) self-raising flour, sifted
100 g (120 ml) castor sugar
100 g butter *or* margarine, softened
1 ml almond essence
2 eggs, beaten
15 g (50 ml) desiccated coconut
14 red glacé cherries, halved
sifted icing sugar to dust (*optional*)

Base
Sift flour into bowl, rub in butter until mixture resembles fine breadcrumbs. Combine castor sugar, egg and milk, beat well.

Make well in centre of flour mixture, add egg mixture, mix to form a soft dough. Spread into greased and lined 320 mm by 240 mm swiss roll pan. Spread jam evenly over dough. Set aside.

Topping
Place all ingredients except coconut and cherries, in a mixing bowl, beat well, two to three minutes. Spread evenly over jam layer, right up to edges of pan. Sprinkle surface evenly with coconut. Press cherries lightly into surface.

Bake at 180 °C, 30 to 35 minutes or until a skewer inserted into the centre comes out clean. Allow to cool in pan, then turn out, remove paper and cut into 28 squares. Dust with icing sugar if desired.

Makes 28.

GINGERBREAD SQUARES

250 g (500 ml) flour, sifted
5 ml ground mixed spice
10 ml ground ginger
90 g (62,5 ml) preserved ginger, finely chopped
45 g (55 ml) golden brown sugar
150 ml milk
125 g butter *or* margarine
125 g (75 ml) treacle
125 g (75 ml) golden syrup
5 ml bicarbonate of soda
1 egg, beaten

TO DECORATE
glacé icing
preserved ginger, finely sliced
glacé cherries, quartered

Sift together dry ingredients. Stir in sugar. Heat milk in a small saucepan, pour into a jug or bowl. Add butter, treacle and golden syrup to same pan, heat until melted. Remove from heat, add to milk. Stir in bicarbonate of soda, add beaten egg. Pour into dry ingredients, beat well.

Turn into a greased and lined, deep-sided 270 mm by 170 mm swiss roll pan, bake at 180 °C, 40 to 45 minutes, or until springy to the touch.

Leave to cool in pan 10 minutes before turning out on to board. Cut into squares, place on wire cooling rack to cool completely. Flavour improves if stored for three to four days before serving. Coat top of each square with glacé icing, decorate with pieces of preserved ginger and glacé cherry. Allow to set before serving.

Makes 25 squares.

Custard raisin squares *(left)*; Fruit bars *(right)*

CUSTARD RAISIN SQUARES

DOUGH
25 g cube fresh yeast
60 g (75 ml) castor sugar
100 ml lukewarm milk
400 g (800 ml) flour, sifted
pinch of salt
50 ml cooking oil
2 large eggs, beaten

TOPPING
250 ml fresh cream
3 large eggs, separated
60 g (75 ml) castor sugar
12,5 ml semolina
90 g (150 ml) seedless raisins

Dough
Cream yeast with 5 ml castor sugar in a small bowl. Stir in milk. Sprinkle 12,5 ml of the flour over surface, cover and leave in warm place until frothy, 15 to 20 minutes.

Sift remaining flour and salt into a large mixing bowl. Make a well in centre, add yeast mixture, remaining castor sugar, oil and beaten eggs. Beat well with wooden spoon until a dough is formed. Turn out on to a lightly floured surface, knead thoroughly until dough is smooth and elastic.

Form into a ball, cover with a greased bowl and leave in a warm, draught-free place until doubled in bulk, about one hour.

Punch down dough, knead well, set aside.

Grease and line a 230 mm by 330 mm swiss roll pan so that sides are at least 50 mm high all the way around.

Roll out dough into a rectangle and line base of prepared pan with dough.

Topping
Lightly beat cream, egg-yolks, castor sugar and semolina together. Whisk egg-whites until soft peaks form. Fold egg-whites and raisins into egg-yolk mixture, spread over dough.

Bake at 200°C, 25 minutes or until custard has set and top is lightly browned.

Remove from oven, leave two minutes in tray, then cut into squares and serve warm with coffee or hot chocolate. Best eaten freshly baked.

Makes 42 squares.

FRUIT BARS

25 g cube fresh yeast
pinch of sugar
125 ml lukewarm milk
250 g (500 ml) flour, sifted
pinch of salt
3 large eggs
125 g (210 ml) prunes, pitted and chopped
60 g (150 ml) dried apple rings, finely chopped
60 g (100 ml) dried pears, finely chopped
125 g (210 ml) dried figs, finely chopped
50 g (90 ml) large seeded raisins, chopped
50 g (90 ml) candied peel, finely chopped
50 g (90 ml) blanched almonds, chopped
5 ml ground cinnamon
finely grated rind of one lemon
100 g dark chocolate, broken into pieces

Cream yeast and sugar in a small bowl, add lukewarm milk, stir well. Sprinkle surface with 12,5 ml of the flour, leave in warm place until frothy, about 15 minutes.

Sift remaining flour and salt into a large mixing bowl, make well in centre. Add yeast mixture and one beaten egg. Mix with wooden spoon, then with hands, until a smooth dough is formed.

Turn out on to a lightly floured surface, knead well. Place in oiled bowl, cover with clingwrap and leave to rise in warm place, about 20 minutes. Turn out again, knead in all the fruit, nuts, spices and lemon rind.

Place chocolate in a bowl over gently simmering water, leave until melted. Remove from heat, stir well until smooth. Add remaining eggs, whisk well.

Add chocolate mixture to dough, continue kneading until all ingredients are well blended. Return to oiled bowl, cover and leave to rise in a warm place, a further 30 minutes.

Turn mixture into a greased 240 mm-square cake pan. Bake at 200°C, about 30 minutes, or until it sounds hollow when rapped with the knuckles.

Turn out on to wire cooling rack, allow to cool completely before cutting into bars.

Makes 32 bars.

SPECIAL OCCASIONS

CUPID'S JAM COOKIES

DOUGH
90 g butter *or* margarine
50 g (60 ml) castor sugar
3 ml vanilla essence
125 g (250 ml) flour, sifted

FILLING
165 g (125 ml) raspberry jam, warmed and sieved
sifted icing sugar

Cream together butter and castor sugar in food processor. Add vanilla essence and sifted flour, process until mixture leaves sides of bowl clean and forms a ball.

Turn out on to a lightly floured surface, knead lightly. Roll out to 3 mm thickness. Cut out rounds using a 55 mm-diameter fluted cutter. Using small heart-shaped cutter, cut out centres of half the rounds.

Place biscuit bases and tops on lightly greased baking trays, bake at 180 °C, eight to 10 minutes, or until pale golden brown. Remove from trays and leave on wire cooling racks to cool.

Spread a little jam over biscuit bases, sandwich together with biscuit tops. Fill heart-shaped centres with more jam. Dust biscuits with sifted icing sugar before serving.

Makes about 15.

LOVER'S PUZZLE

180 g butter *or* margarine, softened
60 g (75 ml) castor sugar
5 ml vanilla essence
60 g (150 ml) hazel-nuts, roasted and ground
250 g (500 ml) flour, sifted
5 ml water *(if necessary)*

TO COMPLETE
white royal icing
200 g dark chocolate, melted

Cream together butter and castor sugar until pale and fluffy. Beat in vanilla essence and ground nuts. Work in sifted flour with wooden spoon or transfer mixture to food processor. Mix well to form a firm dough, adding water if necessary. Wrap in waxwrap and chill in refrigerator about 30 minutes. Roll out between two sheets of greaseproof paper (or use the Doughmaster plastic sheets) into a rectangle 210 mm by 280 mm and about 6 mm thickness. Cut in half, making two puzzles, each 210 mm by 140 mm. Transfer to lightly greased baking tray. Trace off puzzle design, given on p. 86, using a pin. Using very sharp-pointed knife, carefully follow pin markings and cut out pieces without separating them at this stage. Bake at 180 °C, 10 to 15 minutes until pale golden brown. Remove from oven and leave on tray five minutes to

Cupid's jam cookies (top); Lover's puzzle (bottom)

cool slightly. Re-trace jigsaw pieces with knife, separating each piece carefully. Transfer to wire cooling rack and leave to cool completely.

Using fine writing nozzle, outline each piece with white royal icing, leave to dry. Outline again, forming a slightly raised border around each piece. Leave to dry. Fill a piping bag with melted chocolate, snip off very small point and flood surface of each piece with chocolate. Leave to harden. Using fine writing nozzle and white royal icing, pipe message over all 12 jigsaw pieces, so that when jigsaw is put together, the message can be easily read. When completely dry, shuffle the pieces, pack into tissue paper in a pretty box and give to the one you love!

Makes two puzzles.

SWEET HEARTS

190 g butter *or* margarine, cut up
100 g (125 ml) sugar
1 egg
310 g (625 ml) flour, sifted twice

TO DECORATE
500 g (565 ml) icing sugar, sifted
1 ml cream of tartar
3 egg-whites
1 ml almond essence
red powder *or* paste food colouring

Soften butter in food processor, add sugar and process well. Add egg, gradually add flour, mix just until dough forms a firm ball. Turn out on to a floured surface, knead until smooth. Wrap in waxwrap and chill in refrigerator 30 minutes.

Divide dough in half, work with one half at a time. Roll out on a lightly floured surface to 6 mm thickness. Cut out heart shapes, using a 70 mm cutter. Using spatula, carefully transfer biscuits to ungreased baking trays. Repeat with remaining dough. Chill in refrigerator 10 minutes before baking at 160 °C, about 15 minutes or just until edges begin to turn golden brown. Leave to cool on trays one to two minutes before removing to wire cooling racks to cool completely.

To decorate
Sift icing sugar into mixer-bowl. Add cream of tartar, egg-whites and almond essence. Beat very well until a stiff royal icing is formed. Divide into two bowls. Leave one white, colour other a rich red by adding powder or paste until correct colour is created. (You will have to add a fair amount of colouring for this!) Cover both bowls with damp cloths and leave covered until required.

Ice tops of biscuits with either red or white icing, leave to dry thoroughly, preferably overnight. Fill piping-bags fitted with fine writing nozzles, with red and white icing. Pipe message and design on to red-coated biscuits using white icing, and use red icing on white-coated biscuits. Leave to dry completely.

Makes 30 to 40 hearts.

GREEK EASTER BISCUITS

125 g butter *or* margarine, softened
125 g (150 ml) castor sugar
2 egg-yolks
250 g (500 ml) flour, sifted
2 ml ground cinnamon
2 ml gound mixed spice
37,5 ml milk

TOPPING
1 egg-white, lightly frothed
sesame seeds

Cream together butter and castor sugar until pale and fluffy. Add egg-yolks, beat well. Sift in flour, cinnamon and mixed spice, mix to a firm dough with milk. Turn out on to a floured surface, knead until smooth. Wrap in wax-paper and chill in refrigerator at least two hours.

Roll out to 6 mm thickness and cut out 75 mm-diameter rounds with a plain cutter. Place on greased baking trays and brush with egg-white. Sprinkle with sesame seeds and bake at 180 °C, 15 to 20 minutes until golden brown and crisp. Remove to wire cooling racks to cool completely. Store in airtight tin.

Makes about 18.

COLOURFUL BISCUIT RINGS

75 g (125 ml) blanched almonds
350 g (700 ml) flour, sifted
250 g butter *or* margarine
180 g (225 ml) sugar
1 large egg
1 egg-yolk
pinch of salt
5 ml finely grated lemon rind
thick glacé icing coloured pale pink
***nonpareilles* (100s and 1 000s)**

Grind almonds in food processor. Add flour and butter, process until fine crumbs form. Add sugar, egg, egg-yolk, salt and lemon rind, process until a firm dough forms and leaves the sides of the bowl clean. Turn out and knead lightly until smooth. Wrap in wax-paper and chill in refrigerator one hour. Roll out dough on a lightly floured surface to 3 mm thickness. Cut out rounds using a 50 mm-diameter plain cutter, then cut out centres using a 20 mm-diameter plain cutter.

Place rings on greased and lined baking trays and bake at 200°C, about eight minutes until pale golden brown. Remove to wire cooling racks to cool completely.

Sandwich two rings together with icing. Spread top with icing and dip into *nonpareilles*. Leave to dry. Store in airtight tins.

Makes about 50 sandwiched rings.

CUPCAKE NESTS

one-third quantity Colourful biscuit rings dough *(see recipe)*
250 g butter *or* margarine, softened
250 g (300 ml) castor sugar
4 large eggs
250 g (500 ml) flour, sifted
10 ml baking-powder
pinch of salt
5 ml vanilla essence *or* lemon essence

LEMON FROSTING
190 g butter *or* margarine, softened
500 g (565 ml) icing sugar, sifted
2 egg-whites
20 ml fresh lemon juice
10 ml finely grated lemon rind

TO COMPLETE
300 g (940 ml) desiccated coconut
apricot jam, warmed
coloured jelly beans

Prepare dough as given in recipe. Roll out dough on a lightly floured surface to 3 mm thickness. Cut out rounds using a 70 mm-diameter plain cutter. Place on greased and lined baking trays. Bake at 200°C, about eight minutes, until pale and golden brown. Remove to wire cooling racks to cool completely. Set aside.

Cream together butter and castor sugar until pale and fluffy. Add eggs, one at a time, beating well after each addition. Sift flour, baking-powder and salt over creamed mixture, fold in gently. Stir in essence. Spoon mixture into 24 paper cases used to line two patty-pans.

Bake at 200°C, 15 to 20 minutes, until well risen and golden brown. Remove to wire cooling racks to cool completely. Remove paper cases.

Lemon frosting
Place butter, half the icing sugar, egg-whites, lemon juice and rind in mixer-bowl, beat on medium speed until smooth. Gradually beat in remaining icing sugar to achieve a good, spreading consistency.

Turn cupcakes upside-down, coat top and sides generously with lemon frosting. Pierce underside of each with a fork and roll top and sides in coconut until completely coated. Spread prepared biscuits with jam, stand a coconut-coated cupcake on each. Press three coloured jelly beans into top of each nest and serve.

Makes 24.

Cupcake nests *(top)* Greek Easter biscuits *(centre left)*; Colourful biscuit rings *(centre right)*; Sour cream biscuits *(bottom)*

SOUR CREAM BISCUITS

250 g (500 ml) flour, sifted
pinch of salt
200 g butter *or* margarine, cut into pieces
75 ml sour cream

TOPPING
1 egg-yolk, beaten
coloured sugar crystals

Place flour and salt in food processor. Add butter and process until fine crumbs are formed. Gradually add sour cream to form a firm dough. Turn out on to a lightly floured surface. Form into a ball, wrap in wax-paper and chill in refrigerator 30 minutes to one hour.

Roll out dough on a floured surface to about 10 mm thickness. Cut out rounds using a 40 mm-diameter fluted cutter. Brush tops with egg-yolk and sprinkle generously with sugar crystals. Place on greased and lined baking trays, bake at 180°C, 15 minutes until pale golden brown. Remove to wire cooling racks to cool completely. Store in airtight tin.

Makes 25 to 30.

Sweet ravioli biscuits *(left)*; Hazel-nut butter biscuits *(centre)*; Fruity mounds *(right)*

HAZEL-NUT BUTTER BISCUITS

375 g (750 ml) flour, sifted
3 ml baking-powder
pinch of salt
250 g butter *or* margarine, softened
125 g (150 ml) castor sugar
5 ml vanilla essence
1 large egg, beaten
100 g (250 ml) hazel-nuts, finely chopped

TO DECORATE
red and green royal incing

Sift together flour, baking-powder and salt into a large mixing bowl. Rub in butter with fingertips until mixture resembles fine crumbs. Add castor sugar, vanilla essence and egg, blend to form a firm dough. Work in nuts until thoroughly blended.

Wrap dough in clingwrap or wax-paper and chill at least 30 minutes in refrigerator.

Roll out between two sheets of greaseproof or wax-paper (or use Doughmaster sheets) to 4 mm thickness. Using fancy biscuit cutters, cut out shapes as desired. Place on lightly greased baking-trays and bake at 200 °C, eight to 10 minutes until pale golden brown.

Remove to wire cooling racks and leave to cool completely.

Coat with red or green royal icing and leave to dry 24 hours. Store in airtight tin until required.

Makes about 65.

FRUITY MOUNDS

60 g butter *or* margarine, softened
45 g (60 ml) soft brown sugar
1 egg, beaten
125 g (250 ml) flour, sifted
2 ml bicarbonate of soda
3 ml ground cinnamon
60 ml brandy *or* rum *or* milk
125 g (200 ml) sultanas
60 g (100 ml) dates, stoned and chopped
2 slices glacé pineapple, finely chopped
100 g (250 ml) pecan nuts, chopped
60 g (95 ml) glacé cherries, coarsely chopped

Cream together butter and brown sugar until pale and fluffy. Beat in egg. Sift dry ingredients into a bowl. Add half to creamed mixture alternately with brandy. Add remaining dry ingredients to fruit, stir well and add to creamed mixture, mixing until well combined. Spoon about 12,5 ml of mixture on to greased baking-trays and bake at 160°C, 15 minutes until pale golden brown and set. Remove to wire cooling racks to cool completely.

Makes about 30.

SWEET RAVIOLI BISCUITS

DOUGH
125 g butter *or* margarine, softened
100 g (125 ml) sugar
1 egg, beaten
25 ml brandy *or* water
5 ml finely grated lemon rind
5 ml vanilla essence
220 g (440 ml) flour, sifted
60 g (120 ml) cornflour, sifted
2 ml salt

FILLING
60 g (150 ml) dried apricots, finely chopped
130 g (100 ml) smooth apricot jam

TOPPING
sifted icing sugar

STEP-BY-STEP: SWEET RAVIOLI BISCUITS

1 Dough Cream together butter and sugar until pale and fluffy. Beat in egg, brandy, lemon rind and vanilla essence. Sift in dry ingredients.

2 Blend well to form a dough. Turn out on to a lightly floured surface, knead until smooth. Wrap in clingwrap or wax-paper and refrigerate a few hours or overnight.

3 Filling Simmer apricots in a little water, five minutes, drain. Add jam and mix well, set aside.

4 Divide dough in half. Working with one half, roll out on generously floured surface into a large rectangle of 3 mm thickness.

5 Using fluted pastry wheel or sharp knife and ruler, cut dough into 50 mm squares.

6 Place on greased baking trays. Spoon about 3 ml filling into centre of each square.

7 Roll out remaining dough and cut into squares as above. Cover filling with dough squares, wet edges.

8 Press edges to seal.

To complete
Bake at 180°C, 20 to 25 minutes until pale golden brown. Remove to wire cooling racks and leave to cool completely. Store in airtight tin and sift icing sugar generously over biscuits before serving.

Makes 30 to 35.

79

SHORTBREAD

500 g butter, softened
250 g (300 ml) castor sugar
500 g (4 x 250 ml) flour, sifted
250 g (500 ml) cornflour, sifted
castor sugar for dredging

Cream together butter and castor sugar until light and creamy. Work flour and cornflour into mixture to form a dough. Divide in half, place each half on a separate, very lightly greased baking tray. Press down dough, shape into 250 mm-diameter rounds of about 10 mm thickness. Cut each into 16 wedges, prick evenly with a fork.

Bake at 160 °C, about one hour. Remove from oven, dredge with castor sugar. Separate wedges by cutting again while still warm, transfer to wire cooling racks to cool completely. Store in airtight container or wrap securely in cellophane paper.

Makes two rounds, of 16 wedges each.

NOVELTY CHRISTMAS BISCUITS

BASIC DOUGH
190g (375 ml) flour, sifted
3 ml bicarbonate of soda
5 ml cream of tartar
125 g butter *or* margarine, chilled and cut into small pieces
1 egg
100 g (125 ml) sugar
5 ml vanilla essence
3 ml finely grated lemon rind

Sift together flour, bicarbonate of soda and cream of tartar into a bowl. Rub in butter until mixture resembles fine breadcrumbs. Set aside.

In another bowl beat egg, sugar, vanilla essence and lemon rind well. Stir into flour mixture to form a firm dough. Refrigerate three hours.

Roll out dough on a lightly floured surface to about 6 mm thickness. Cut out Christmas shapes using bought cutters or trace off designs given on pp. 82-84. Cut a 6 mm-diameter hole in each biscuit to facilitate hanging. Using spatula, carefully transfer biscuits to lightly greased baking trays.

Bake at 180 °C, 10 to 12 minutes. Leave to cool on trays one to two minutes before removing to wire cooling racks to cool completely.

Makes 25 to 30 biscuits.

ROYAL ICING
3 egg-whites
500 g (565 ml) icing sugar, sifted

Whip egg-whites lightly, gradually add icing sugar, 12,5 ml at a time, beating continuously five to 10 minutes until icing resembles well-beaten cream and forms stiff, glossy peaks. Keep covered with damp cloth until required.

TO DECORATE
red, yellow and green powder *or* paste food colouring
No 1 or 2 plain writing nozzle
greaseproof paper piping bags
silver balls
red, yellow and green ribbon

1 Place one biscuit at a time upside-down on table fork, dip into icing to coat one side (leave a few biscuits uncoated). Allow excess icing to drip off, turn biscuit upright on to your hand, slide on to wire cooling rack to dry, about 15 minutes.

2 Divide remaining icing into three small bowls, colour one red, one yellow and one green.

Wreaths Using green icing and plain writing nozzle, pipe outline around outer and inner rim of biscuit and use red to pipe around tie. Leave to dry.

3 Fill tie area with red dots and pipe a row of green dots between rims. Place a silver ball on every alternate green dot. Leave to dry.

4 **Stocking** Pipe red icing on to biscuit as shown. Leave to dry.

5 Complete decoration with an outline of green icing.

To complete
Decorate the various shaped biscuits with royal icing as shown in photograph. Leave to dry. Insert ribbon through hole and hang biscuits on the Christmas tree on Christmas morning. (Keep stored in airtight container until required or they may go soft.)

82

83

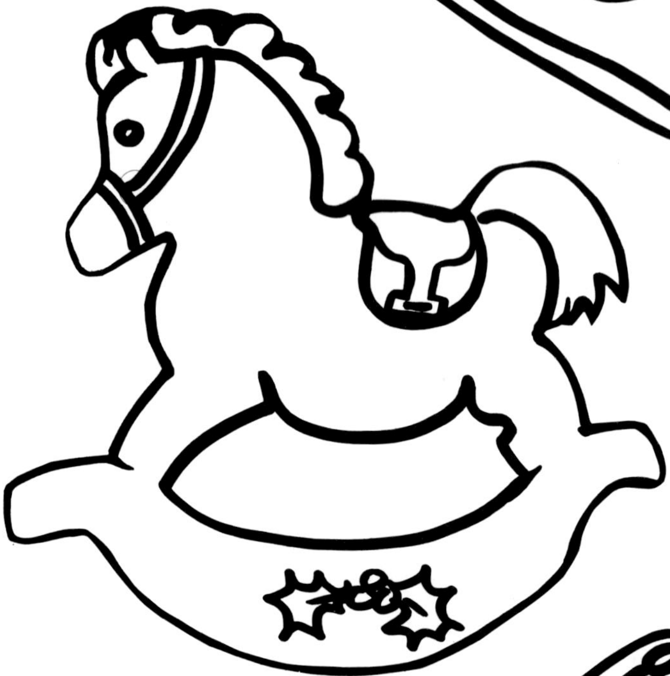

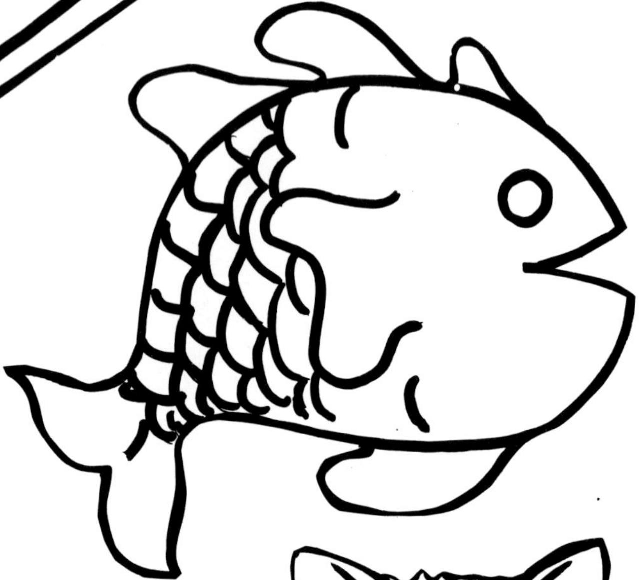

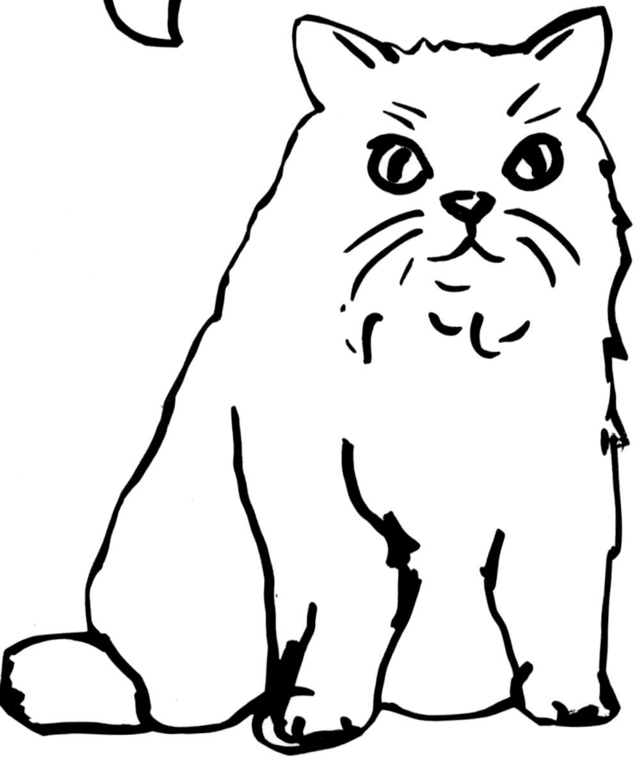

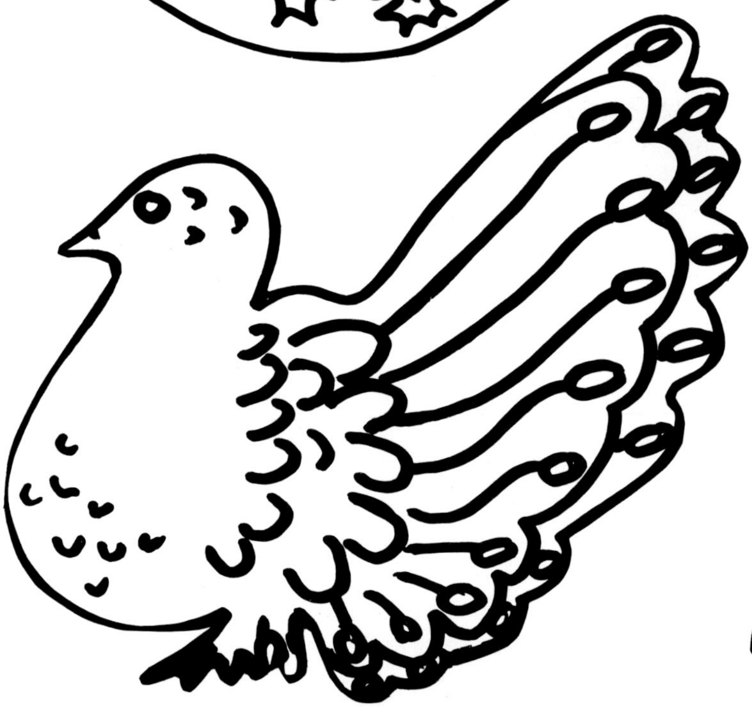

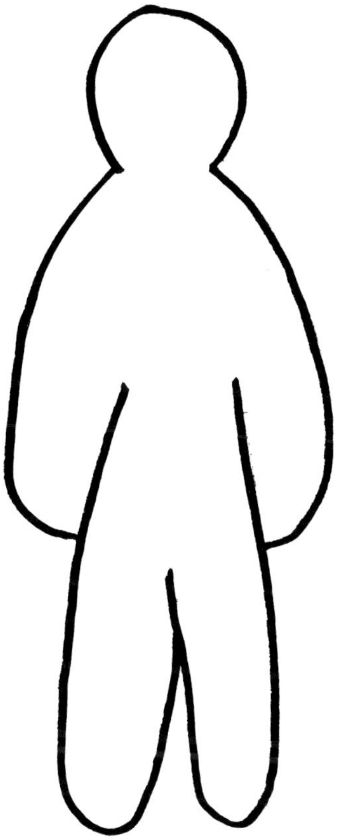

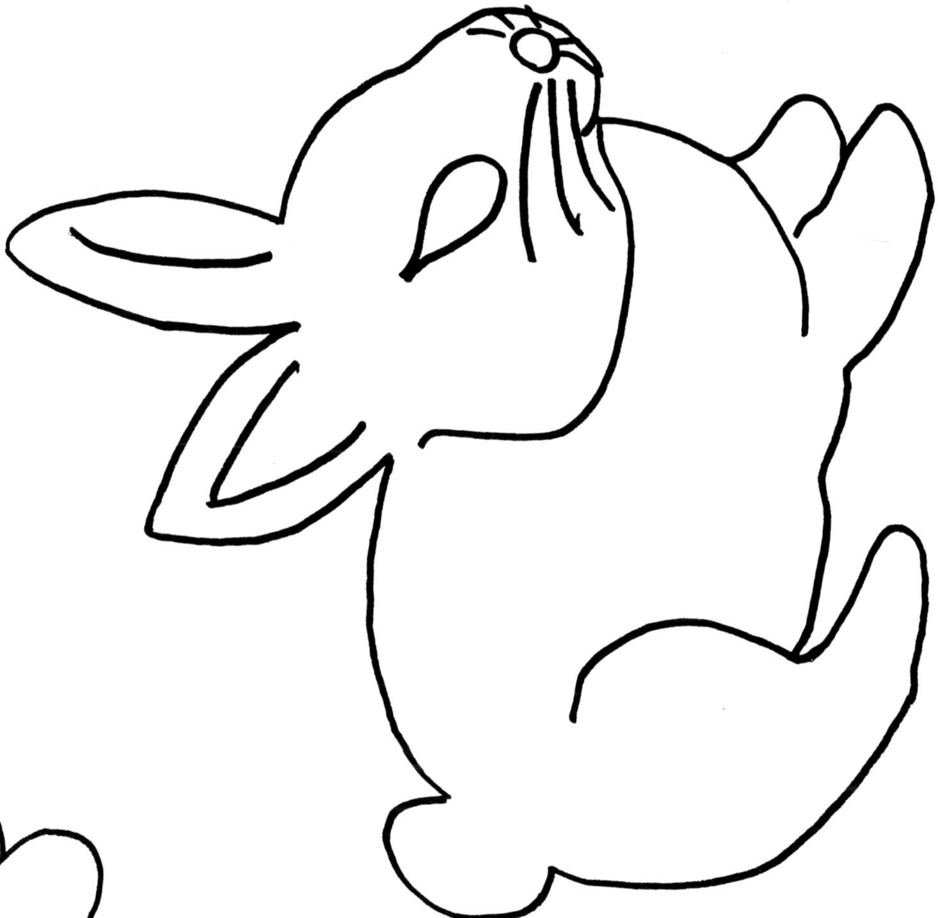

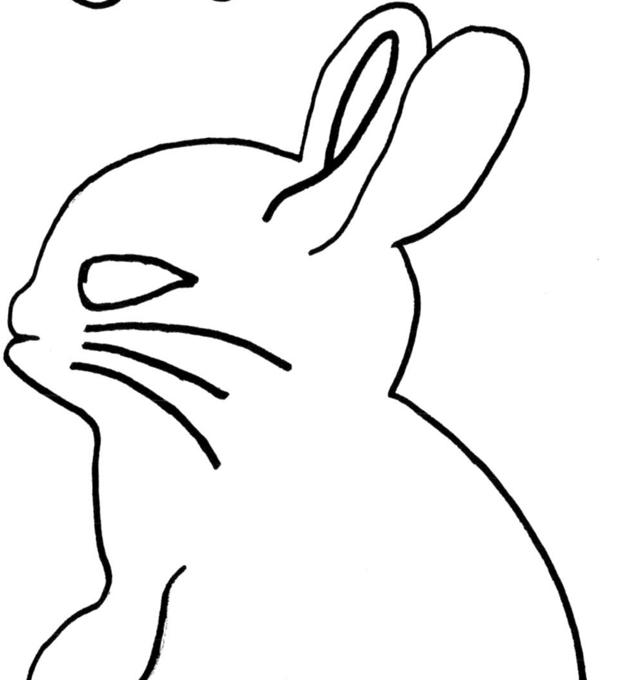

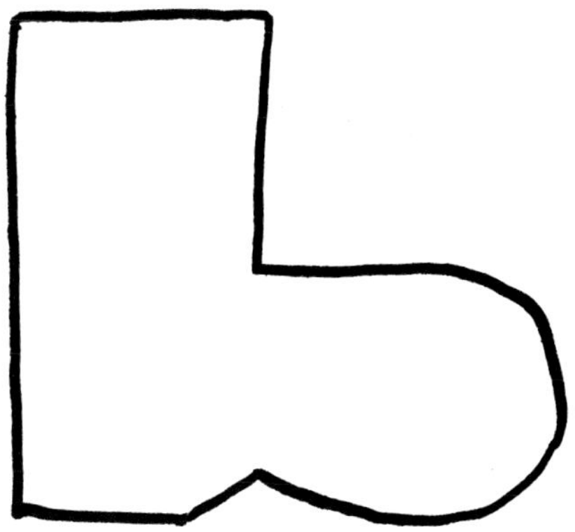

ALPHABETICAL RECIPE INDEX

Afghans, 71
Almond and pecan puffs, 52
– cherry and nut, 12
– and chocolate cookies, 31
– coconut slices, 68
– crescents, 50
– fruit slice, 55
– whirls, 53
Apple and almond squares, 65
– sauce bars, 72
Apricot pastry pretzels, 21
– rings, 19

Bakewell bars, 19
Banana pecan squares, 72
Boot biscuits, 39
Busy Lizzies, 32
Butter biscuits, step-by-step, 10
– finger biscuits, 7

Caramel biscuits, 9
Cherry buttons, 10
– garlands, 15
– shells, 28
– shells, 29
Chewy nut bars, 70
Chip biscuits, 13
Choc-chip cookies, 56
– monster cookies, 43
Choc–wheat biscuits, 57
Chocolate and vanilla spirals, 56
– and almond squares, 10
– and orange marbles, 15
– cherry wedges, 17
– dip biscuits, 48
– fridge roll, 16
– melts, 29
– mint buttons, 15
– orange cookies, 56
– shorties, 28
– wheels with nuts, 47
Cinnamon biscuits, 34
– snaps, 13
Coconut and almond squares, 72
– melting moments, 65
Coffee hazel-nut biscuits, 62
– and pecan-nut biscuits, 59
– cream biscuits, 60
– cream filling, 60
– finger biscuits, 60
– kisses, 60
Colourful biscuit rings, 76
Cookie-press butter biscuits, 40
Creamy lemon dreams, 46
Crisp and creamy chocolate surprises, 58
Crispy cheese biscuits, 64
– chocolate fingers, 69
– diagonals, 16
Crunchy biscuits, 41

– chocolate biscuits, 69
– chocolate bars, 6
– lemon drops, 28
Cupcake nests, 77
Cupid's jam cookies, 75
Custard raisin squares, 74
– kisses, 12

Danish blue bites, 63
Date and biscuit squares, 17
– chews, 23
Date-nut ribbons, 15
Deep-fried raspberry rosettes, 22

Florentines, step-by-step, 25
Fruit and nut rounds, 26
– bars, 74
– -mince delights, 6
Fruit-cake bars, 23
Fruity mounds, 79

Gingerbread boys and girls, 39
– squares, 73
Greek Easter biscuits, 76

Hawaiian biscuits, 8
Hazel-nut butter biscuits, 78
Honey almond biscuits, 54

Iced fancies, 20
– giant cookies, 43

Juggler's cheese sticks, 64
Jam daisies, 10

Kisses from Holland, 8

Lemon and granadilla twists, 49
Lollipop biscuits, 41
Lover's puzzle, 75

Macaroons, 52
Mandarin orange biscuits, 49
Marshmallow biscuits, 66
– rings, 41
Marzipan fancies, 23
Mealie-meal biscuits, 68
Melting orange creams, 29

No-bake oat biscuits, 16
Novelty Christmas biscuits, 80
Nutty chocolate squares, 55
– lemon slices, 44

Orange and ginger biscuits, 36
– brandy creams, 22
– creams, 13
– stars, 28

Pecan caramel chickens, 17
– cornflake cookies, 70
Pineapple sandwich crunchies, 70
Piped biscuits, 27
– chocolate biscuits, 30
– delights, 29
– vanilla rosettes, 30
Praline creams, 53
– delights, 50
Pressed ginger biscuits, 37
– cookies, 31

Quick-mix biscuits, 15

Rabbit biscuits, 39
Raisin walnut cookies, 26

Savoury cheese biscuits, 63
Scoop biscuits, 8
Seed biscuits, 70
Shortbread, 80
Shrewsbury biscuits, 12
Silky chocolate squares, 57
Sour cream biscuits, 77
– raisin biscuits, 12
Spangles, 15
Sparkling sugar stars, 40
Spiced oatmeal drops, 33
Strawberry and cinnamon shorties, 19
Sugar pretzels, 10
Sugared knots, 15
Sunny circles, 15
Super oatmeal cookie, 43
Sweet hearts, 76
– ravioli biscuits, step-by-step, 79

Tangy mustard nibbles, 64
Thumb cookies, 21

Vanilla rounds, 48
Viennese fingers, 28